D0438133

NATIONAL GEOGRAPHIC DIRECTIONS

ALSO BY WILLIAM KITTREDGE

Southwestern Homelands

WILLIAM KITTREDGE

Southwestern Homelands

NATIONAL GEOGRAPHIC DIRECTIONS

NATIONAL GEOGRAPHIC
Washington D.C.

Published by the National Geographic Society
1145 17th Street, N.W., Washington, D.C. 20036-4688

Library of Congress Cataloging-in-Publication Data

    Kittredge, William.
      Southwestern Homelands / William Kittredge
         p. cm.—(National Geographic directions)
      ISBN 0-7922-6534-3
      1. Southwest, New–Description and travel. 2. Kittredge,
    William–Journeys–Southwest, New–History. I. Title II. Series.

    F787 .K54 2002
    979–dc21
                      2002019349

Book design by Michael Ian Kaye and Tuan Ching, Ogilvy & Mather, Brand Integration Group

Printed in the U.S.A

For the true traveling companion,
Annick Smith

CONTENTS

Southwestern Homelands

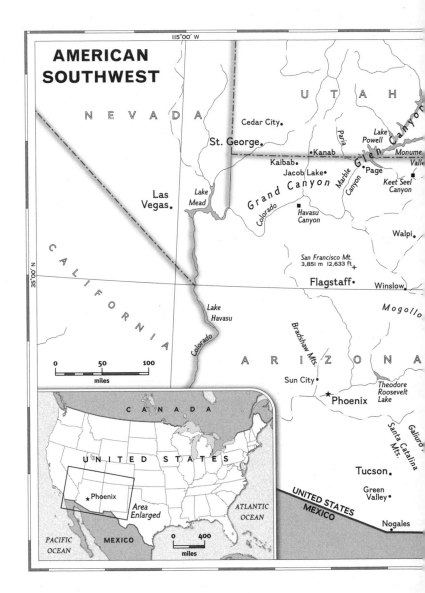

AMERICAN SOUTHWEST

115°00' W

N E V A D A

U T A H

Cedar City.

•Kanab

St. George.

Paria

Lake Powell

Monume Vall

Kaibab•

Jacob Lake•

•Page

Keet Seel Canyon

Las Vegas.

Lake Mead

Grand Canyon

Marble Canyon

Glen Canyon

Colorado

Havasu Canyon

Walpi•

C A L I F O R N I A

San Francisco Mt.
3,851 m 12,633 ft

Flagstaff•

Winslow.

35°00' N

Lake Havasu

M o g o l l o

Colorado

Bradshaw Mts.

A R I Z O N A

0   50   100
miles

Sun City •

Theodore Roosevelt Lake

★ Phoenix

Santa Catalina Mts.

Galiuro

Tucson.

Green Valley •

Nogales

C A N A D A

U N I T E D   S T A T E S

★Phoenix

Area Enlarged

ATLANTIC OCEAN

PACIFIC OCEAN

MEXICO

UNITED STATES
MEXICO

0   400
miles

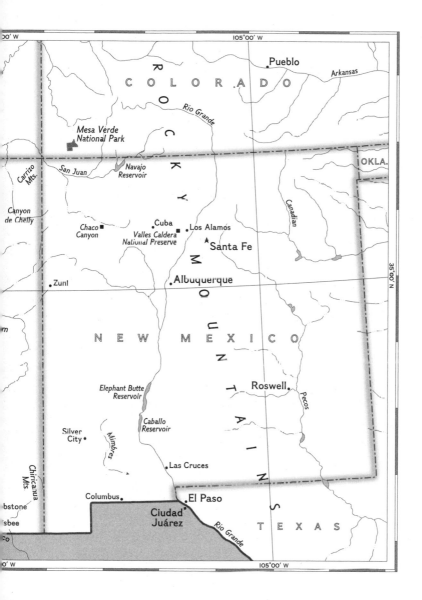

Pueblo

Arkansas

C O L O R A D O

R

O

Rio Grande

Mesa Verde
National Park

C

San Juan

Navajo
Reservoir

Carrizo Mts.

K

OKLA.

Canyon
de Chelly

Chaco
Canyon

Cuba

Los Alamos

Valles Caldera
National Preserve

Y

Canadian

Santa Fe

35°00′ N

Zuni

Albuquerque

M

O

U

N E W   M E X I C O

N

Elephant Butte
Reservoir

Roswell

T

Pecos

Caballo
Reservoir

A

Silver
City

Mimbres

I

Las Cruces

N

Chiricahua Mts.

bstone

sbee

Columbus

El Paso

S

Ciudad
Juárez

Rio Grande

T E X A S

Preface

> *Every continent has its own spirit of place.*
> *Every people is polarized in some particular locality,*
> *which is home, the homeland.*
>
> D. H. LAWRENCE
> *Studies in Classic American Literature*

At the trailhead, waiting for the man with the horses, we were stunned by light, the yellow-white needles of the cholla backlit by sunrise, abruptly luminous. So this was the Sonoran Desert.

Annick and I were going for a day in the Superstition Mountains, a range which rises abruptly in a line of dark basalt cliffs at the eastern edge of the Phoenix metroplex. We were there with the attorney general of Arizona, a man obsessed with rediscovering the Lost Dutchman Mine, a legendary vein of gold-bearing quartz. Examples of that quartz existed. They were fabulous, thick with clots of gold. But all idea of the mine's location died with the man who found it. Searching in the Superstitions was the attorney general's hobby. Because of my childhood, I was sympathetic.

My grandfather on my mother's side came of age in a mining camp. Having run off from his father's farm in Wisconsin, by the age of fourteen he was "sharpening steel"—picks and pry-bars—working as a blacksmith in Butte, Montana. He wandered to "Old Mexico," and up to Goldfield and Rhyolite in Nevada before settling and marrying in Grants Pass, Oregon, where he and a brother opened a blacksmith and horse-shoeing shop. But that failed and most of his working life was spent blacksmithing for COPCO, the California-Oregon Power Company. His name was Al Miessner, and he was the most openhanded man I've known.

When I was a boy I'd follow Al up the alley behind the house on Jefferson Street in Klamath Falls where he lived with my grandmother, to the door of a remodeled garage where a mining-camp pal of his, a man crippled deep underground, lived a sort of hermit's life. They'd sip bottles of home brew and talk about the runaway boys they'd been. "Too young to know a damned thing. Or care." The old crippled man would struggle to stand, raise his bottle, and curse the mines, and Al would smile. They had known heroic times. What to say? My heart breaks for them, so long dead, and for me, without them.

So, having grown up on stories like those, and because of the example of my parents, who were bravehearted in their own ways, I yearned to take part in legendary doings. But no such luck in the Superstitions. No gold. We had a semi-gourmet camp lunch, in the shade of great-armed saguaro cactus instead.

Not long after, I was in a room with mountaineers who were asked to tell us what they thought they were doing as they roped up to risk their being on perpendicular stone walls in the vastnesses of the Alps and the Rockies and the Andes and Asian ranges. They surprised their audience by talking about intimacy, about being at home on the rock faces, and staying happy on the endorphins generated by their bodies. As I understand it, they were talking about drifting and dreaming, nomadic leaning and learning, and how all can be a continual move toward home.

CHAPTER ONE

Going South

Going south is a pervasive notion in the northern Rockies, where I live. It has to do with fleeing winter. Often we go to the American Southwest, arid lands bounded by the watersheds of the Colorado and Rio Grande Rivers.

Seeking warmth and sunlight in a land where spicy food, music, and frivolity are understood to be ordinary human needs, our mood lifts as we go. Flight involves a spot of reinventing the sweet old psychic self.

Our species evolved on the run. Part of us yearns constantly toward nomadism; we're emotionally hardwired to every once in a while hit the road. As my old pal, the poet Richard Hugo, said, "The car that brought you here still runs."

It's an ancient dream: Walk out, and as you go listen while the world in its intricacy sings and hums. The child on its mother's hip listens as she moves on through the world, and speaks the names. In the Southwest her litany might go "badger, quail in flight from the bosque, cotton fields, ocotillo, coyote skull, mudhead kachina, roadrunner, expressway."

Entering my seventh decade, I usually opt for quiet pleasures and diversions. No more nonstop drinking and driving. I like to contemplate the stars and planets surrounding a cup of moon in the night sky over Arizona. Or ease along the banks of Cave Creek, below the reddish cliffs on the eastern edge of the Chiricahua Mountains, in the quick presence of hummingbirds. I want to unreservedly love my beloved, and fool aimlessly around while it's still possible.

At the same time, without purposes we wither. So it's useful to understand that travel is not altogether an indulgence. Going out, seeking psychic and physical adventures, can reawaken love of the shifting presence of the sacred Zen "ten thousand things" we find embodied in the wriggling world. Travel, then, is a technique for staying in touch, a wake-up call, not a diversion but a responsibility.

Journeying is ideally a move toward reeducation, but it's also a try at escape from our insistent homebound selves, from boredom or from too much to do, not enough quietude, from the mortal coil of who we've lately been.

Where were you last night?

Out.

What were you running from?

Mechanical civilization, I want to say, and its sources of discontent, the Stuck on the Wheel of Repetition Disorder, or Temporary Blindness, or what might be called the Yearning for Other Points of View and Variety Anxiety.

Overwhelmed by the intricacy of our relationships, we turn resentful and cranky, constantly aware of what's called "the bastard unfairness of things." There come times when we dream of afternoons reading on a veranda overlooking Mediterranean islands or a mountain lake. Or fantasize about nights spent dancing down Bourbon Street with strangers.

We're not by nature always entirely at ease with nonstop domesticity. (I'm not advocating infidelity; what I've got in mind are other forms of psychic renewal.) Don't mistake me. The virtues of a rooted life are real. It's just that, as with agriculture, they can be practiced too intensively and deplete the soils.

In the Southwest, where it's natural to study distances fading into distances, landforms are almost impossible to ignore. Multicolored badlands and dark mountain ranges rising from the arid flatlands like islands and intricate water curved gorges are insistently present in the stories travelers tell of where they've been and where they're going.

Dinosaurs fed and bred and roamed beside a shallow sea with marshy shores and beaches where sand collected in wind-and-water-driven swirling patterns. The sea dried up and the fossilized bones of the dinosaurs, along with petrified trees and seashells, hardened into limestone ridges. Millions of years passed as the dunes compacted into the swirling reefs of sandstone we see in the walls of the Grand Canyon and Canyon de Chelly, then eroded into the towers of Monument Valley or the mesas where the Hopi live.

At least 150 million years ago, the North American plate began breaking off from Europe, drifting west, to collide with the Pacific plate. One sank, the other rose—the Pacific plate was driven into the earth's hot liquid mantle as the North American plate reared over it. The result was mountain building, known as the Laramide orogeny—aka the Rocky Mountains and the Sierra Nevada—which formed a barrier and cast a rain shadow. Damp air from the Pacific rose and stalled, rain fell over those mountains, but the lands beyond to the east, our Southwest, left to dry winds, evolved into deserts.

The most basic physical fact human settlement runs up against in the Southwest is aridity. Drought and rain dances of so many kinds testify to the constant need for conservation. Cities like Phoenix and Tucson and Albuquerque evolved in conjunction with adequate (so far) water.

The Earth's crust lifted and stretched, and a five-hundred-mile north-south rift valley was formed in what's now New Mexico. Streams eventually collected in the Rio Grande. At roughly the same time the vast highlands of the 130,000-square-mile Colorado Plateau rose in northern Arizona and northwestern New Mexico. The Colorado River eroded down through the stratas of sandstone into the ultimate ancient black schist, creating the Grand Canyon. There's a ridge across north-central Arizona, where the highland deserts of the Colorado Plateau fall off two thousand feet, which is known as the Mogollon Rim (Muggy-OWN). To the south and into Mexico lies Basin and Range Country—vast, shimmering creosote flatlands, salty and arid, and high timbered mountains, the Santa Ritas, the Chiricahuas, the Santa Catalinas.

So, a lost inland sea, a collision of plates, a rain shadow, a highland plateau, isolated rivers cutting through reefs of sandstone, islands of mountains in lowland deserts, fields of lava, tracts of shifting white sands—the Southwest can be thought of as shape-shifting.

My first trip to the Southwest, in the spring of 1969, was for me a time of discovery. We'd sold the cattle ranch where I grew up in the Great Basin "cold desert" country of southeastern Oregon—lava rock and sagebrush—and I was launched into another life. I dreamed of William Faulkner and tried to reinvent myself in classes at "the famous Writers' Workshop" at the University of Iowa, where stress levels were running high by mid-March. It was time to run for sunlight. A friend from Oregon, William Roecker, was teaching at the University of Arizona in Tucson. I took him up on an invitation to visit.

We went immediately to a biker bar called the Poco Loco, on Speedway in Tucson, and played pinball alongside giant tattooed fellows who were amiable enough until I tripped over a cord and unplugged a machine. In this way, a daylong effort to accumulate hundreds of free games was lost. My very life seemed in jeopardy until it was decided by a very judicious daddy with a mane of tangled gray hair that it wasn't my fault since I was clearly a fool and not to be held responsible.

"Forget it. This ninny don't know where he is." I was judged to be dumb as a spare tire. So I carried my can of beer outside and sat on the steps and sulked.

Foolishness aside, a couple of other phenomena, when reflected upon in tranquillity, quite turned my head. The first was a Gila monster. Driving across the deserts to the Kitt Peak National Observatory, Bill Roecker slammed on the brakes and we swayed to an emergency stop. After walking back a couple hundred yards we found a Gila monster, poisonous enough to be lethal, nearly two feet long, a rough old customer, scales on his heavy body blotched and broken into spots of black, yellow, and orange, a dangerous nighttime creature, and near the high-way in daylight, tongue flicking, tasting our air. It seemed important to focus on this creature closely. But the monster was utterly alien. I tried to look but could not see. I had difficulty remembering any details a week or so later. Touching was unthinkable, as was sitting down and getting used to that lizard's otherness.

This dysfunction, the Failure to Experience, is common among travelers, is often also called Paralyzed by Expectations. Seeing comes easier to those who are calmly unworried, like skaters on hard ice who are only skating, flowing along and not in the least conscious of style or trying to reinvent.

But, semi-blind, I at least understood that surprises were what I was there for, and unlikely unless actively sought after, courted. I was thirty-six years old and had never been to a place so foreign as this; maybe another version of my life was beginning.

The next move, almost immediately, was on to another country, Mexico. We tried the after-dark pleasures of Nogales, but the memorable episode came during a fishing trip to Guaymas on the Mexican coast, three big boys doing a Huck

Finn imitation, running to territory, hoping to be scandalous but not seriously. We rented a skiff with an outboard motor, trolled the bay, and caught innumerable mackerel. At first it was routine, the baiting and hooking, fishing.

But, then, the utterly singular. Gray whales rose around us, dozens of gray whales. I have no idea what they were doing— feeding, flirting, whatever—a great sighing and seawater splashing through rainbows, creatures rising on all sides until it was possible to think of them as extraordinary but nevertheless natural, not at all miraculous.

So this was the sort of thing that could happen, encounters with evolving actual real-life otherness. I'd never seen anything like those whales. The world, the whole all-over-the-place, reeked and was more various than I'd ever before been driven to imagine.

Bill Roecker eventually gave up writing poetry. After a pretty good book was published, he quit. He's now a deep-sea fisherman on the coast north of San Diego. I've always admired the fact that he was willing to turn away from what he'd thought he was supposed to do—write poems every morning— and devote himself to what he loved, Fishing.

In the 1970s, on the weekend of St. Patrick's Day, I trooped along with quickly aging pals on the hillside streets of the tough old empire city in the northern Rockies, the deep-mine town of Butte. What were we seeking? "Wateringholes," someone said, "like in Africa, where animals congregate."

But the fun turned predictable and repetitive. The animals and wateringholes were not so interesting as they had been.

Maybe we, ourselves, were boring. It took awhile, but we finally acknowledged that possibility. What to do about it? Who knew? Maybe we were getting too old for fun. Was it possible to outgrow pleasure? Was that the problem with old grouchy people? The answers here, of course, are no, no, and no. My father told jokes and laughed a week before he died of system failure and agonies at eighty-nine. Maybe it's just that the venues change.

In 1976 I started going to conferences focused on western problems. I'd spent a decade carousing and it was time for a change; I wanted desperately to get in on some serious intellectual action. At Sun Valley, prize-winning historians like Alvin Josephy and William Goetzmann sat in the front row studying me with what I took to be suspicion one July morning as I stood up and spent my allotted seven minutes pushing the concept that the American West as commonly understood was a manufactured story that could and should—if the West was ever to emotionally and intellectually own itself—be retold. While I thought I was breaking new ground, it was a line those scholars no doubt found familiar. But they were kind. They included me in lunchtime discussions and recommended books. Another education began.

In the fall of 1978 a man named Terry McDonell, an editor and a grand one—I was having a run of luck—called and asked if I'd write an essay for a new publication called *Rocky Mountain Magazine.* I didn't know how to write an essay, but Terry told me how on the telephone and got me through a little piece called "Redneck Secrets." Which he published. So then I was an essayist, and I'd found a new form in which I could shoot off my mouth, one that seemed to fit better than the fiction I'd been producing at the rate of about a story a year for the last decade. I was at last getting my act sort of together after suffering a run of self-made defeat, including divorces that were my own damned fault.

It was a brave, happy time, most of all because I had a new love, Annick Smith, who has been my life's companion from then until now. She'd just raised the money to produce a film called *Heartland*. So, riding a wave, Annick and I put the miss on St. Patrick's Day. We headed south on Interstate 15, to Salt Lake City and the unknown but warm and welcoming Southwest.

We made the five hundred miles to Salt Lake City by dark, and ate an elegant meal in the Cafe Santa Fe in Emigration Canyon, the food semi-exotic and far better than we were used to. We were absolutely and at last on the road. Thank you, Mister Kerouac, for your example.

In southern Utah, below Cedar City on our way to St. George, after hours of traversing snowy March highlands, I-15 topped a long swale scattered with juniper trees. What the locals call Mormon Dixie—looming blue skies, a yellowish rather than gray landscape, exotic red rock canyons, warmth— opened out before and below us as if a curtain had been pulled.

This was what we came to call The Gateway to the South. There lay the salty land where snow didn't stick, where winter didn't live. But what now? Zion National Park, with its red-rock walls, and sweet trail weaving through aspen beside the brook which becomes the Virgin River, was there at hand. But we didn't go to Zion, not that trip. One thing we knew; we were headed Way Farther South.

I wanted to go where snow was only a theory, where people had heard about it, where they loved the idea of snowmen but hadn't actually had an opportunity to drive isolated highways into a blinding blizzard. I knew for sure that winter nights go on too long in Montana. I was looking for a place where the sun came up earlier and went down later.

We wanted to be canny travelers but didn't know how. We'd highlighted and underlined in a couple of guidebooks, but we hadn't learned much beyond abstractions. We didn't know why the Hopi and the Chiricahua Apache were different, or the difference between Sedona and Green Valley. We didn't know why the skies before us were cloudless and likely to remain that way most of the time. We blundered but nevertheless had a swell time.

Just into Arizona, hordes of girls in bright pinafores, yellow and green and pinkish red, seemed both happy and subdued as they traipsed hand in hand on clean streets in Colorado City, a town of multifamily homes where polygamy flourishes. Those children seemed to have emerged straight from a 1940s Judy Garland movie about the virtues of small-town life. Except they never started dancing and singing.

On down the road, at Pipe Spring National Monument, the headquarters for what had been an enormous Mormon frontier ranch, we wandered through a stonework ranch house built to double as a fortress where settlers defended themselves with weapons. Slots through which rifles could be fired at invaders were built into the kitchen walls.

South of Kanab, where so many Westerns were filmed, I had opened a long tradition of Utah speeding tickets. It seemed unjust. I'd been drifting and dreaming on an undulating highway built for velocity.

At Jacob Lake, in the forested highlands of the Kaibab Plateau, the north entrance to the Grand Canyon National Park was drifted with snow and closed for winter. So I've never stood on the north edge of that abyss. Which, according to reputable testimony, is absolutely my loss.

Page Stegner writes of hiking to Widforss Point in order to witness an "endless cacophony of buttes, buttresses, points, pyramids, terraces, and cathedrals soaring out of the 'awesome cavity' that defies narration." Stegner says it would be easier to describe the excellent and complex wine he drank on the spot, and quotes Clarence Dutton, the earliest geologist to study the Kaibab and the canyon, who says, "All these attributes combine with infinite complexity to produce a whole which at first bewilders and at length overpowers." What's natural, of course, when studied closely, because of accumulated infinities, often produces that effect.

But Annick and I plunged down to House Rock Valley (where people had lived in rooms fashioned under the sides of boulders), a flat which breaks off into the Marble Canyon of the Colorado. Above us the Vermilion Cliffs were a stone reef adrift in twilight ocher.

On the narrow old highway bridge above Marble Canyon, high above the river, gazing into those stony darkening depths, I imagined leaping, falling into a dream of tumbling and tumbling. Here, the actual item—the clear possibility of simply jumping—and fantasy were juxtaposed. The invasion of reality, as someone said of Borges's stories, by dream. *Calm down,* I told myself, *look around, breathe.*

Give me that old rock and roll, the unbroken circle. All I had to do was vanish into breathing and seeing. *This,* a voice whispered, *is it.*

But what? This is *what?* I didn't know. Before me lay "timelessness," if eternity is a thing, another gateway—but one I didn't for sure want to enter. What to do? Get off that bridge. I was overstimulated—experiencing too much, seeing altogether too freshly. Enough with the proximity of psychic transitions. How about dinner?

Solace took the form of a fisherman's motel near the rim. There's splendid trout fishing in the dozen miles below the otherwise abominable Glen Canyon Dam; deep water released from the reservoir is cold, and trout thrive. After a supper of baked trout and homemade macaroni-and-cheese served by a Navajo woman who sang a song in her own language as she brought us apple pie adorned with vanilla ice cream, I slept like a child.

The next morning we breakfasted amid jolly fishermen, a crew of boasting, boisterous old boys and sixtyish sun-dark wives who seemed to be semipermanent local residents in a village of travel trailers. Then we drove down onto the alluvial fan where the Paria River emerges from the chambers of its fantasyland canyon to join the Colorado. We found another gateway.

A sloping concrete launch ramp was thronging with adventurers—bronzed and sometimes profoundly cool young men and women in black skin-tight Lycra, and twitchy, dumpy midlife men and women with guidebooks, and lean knowing oldsters—all about to launch themselves onto the river. Fat men and weight lifters, very old aristocratic women—pilgrims, a carnival of river rats, both the experienced and the apprentice. The air rang with the clatter of aluminum on concrete and shouts and catcalls. Great gray motorized rafts and occasional one-person kayaks and six-seat rowing dories were being loaded for expeditions into the layered stone depths and lapping silences. Annick was deep into fantasies about running the Grand Canyon. Since then she's gone twice, and will go again, given twenty minutes to prepare.

But right then I was more interested in the story of John Doyle Lee, and his role in the Mountain Meadows Massacre, in which an entire wagon train was slaughtered. Lee had spent decades running his ferry across the Colorado, and his stone house and orchard are still there, just inland from the boat ramp.

During the hard summer of 1857, a wagon train bound for southern California came down through the settlements of Utah, raiding gardens and herds, living off what food they could steal. This drove the Mormon settlers to ambush and kill all of them but those children too young to remember. Why, we wonder, this astonishing response?

D. H. Lawrence wrote, "The savage America was conquered and subdued at the expense of instinctive and intuitive sympathy of the human soul. The fight was too brutal." History tells us merciless stories about the costs of finding and taking over some promised land or another.

After that terrifying afternoon, John Doyle Lee was sent by the Mormon Church to run the ferry deep in this canyon, the only viable place within two hundred miles to cross the big river. Lee lived there with his family until, two decades later, he was tried in Cedar City, taken to the site of the massacre, and shot by a firing squad. Among mature pear trees, I found a gray withered limb, carried it out, and keep it yet, to remind me of where we can be led by yearnings and true belief.

Carrying my limb, I wandered to the trailhead where hikers can head up into the deep confines of the ribbonlike canyon carved by the Paria River. A lean midlife man in shorts and heavy-duty hiking boots was loading a worn backpack. Turned out he wrote guidebooks, and didn't want much to do with greenhorns like me.

"What are you going to do?" I asked.

"Be careful."

"How long are you going to be gone?"

"A few days. But I'm not gone."

Back in the car, on the road again, I couldn't stop thinking about that man. He was deliberately seeking isolation. If I went, what would I find? Maybe silence, eternities, and myself among them, with no voices to listen to but the ones in my head. Was that a good idea? Maybe I'd emerge half-crazed and singing "Why don't you love me like you used to do" in a loud way, having turned into one of those people who play the radio or CDs and talk on their cell phones and laugh constantly so as to fill the air with something besides what they're thinking.

CHAPTER TWO

Mutual Enterprise

Discoveries were accumulating. In the summer of 1981 I was asked to write an essay about a fellow filming grizzly bears in Glacier National Park, a couple of hours north of Missoula, where I live. "Doug Peacock. He'll be in the bar at the Belton Chalet at three o'clock tomorrow afternoon."

A couple of pilgrims had been killed by a grizzly bear at a campsite on the banks of St. Mary Creek, just outside the park. I said I didn't know anything about grizzly bears.

"Don't worry about it. He's the ace."

What kind of ace?

"He's the underground hero of grizzly bear stuff. He'll take you right out there, to the bears, close up."

I said I didn't want anything close-up to do with grizzlies. I mean, in theory, I understood that they were one of nature's terrific ideas. "He's the man," the editor said. *"The,* get it, *man."*

"Peacock?" The bartender was a huge hippie-biker fellow named Dave. "Shit," Dave said, "Peacock might not show up for days. Peacock might be dead."

Then the evening sun was setting over West Glacier. I'd been waiting for my appointment with Peacock for hours and I was close to *very* drunk.

Just in time, through the screen door, there came voices, confusion, and the yapping of huge dogs. Big Dave the friendly bartender grinned at me. "Here's your man," he said. And there they came, in from their afternoon amid the forests and animals, seeking drink, the legendary men, Peacock and his old buddy from the Sonoran Desert, Edward Abbey, who helped make Peacock legendary while shaping his own legend.

In *The Monkey Wrench Gang,* Abbey created a band of environmental outlaws engaged in war against greedy, dimwit, and use-oriented assholes who would tear up our holy earth in order to build another raft of tract houses, or a shopping center, or expand another airport, or sink a run of canyonland under water behind another hydroelectric dam. The character who came alive, the most energetic, imaginative, and revolutionary of them all, a reckless mountain-man intellectual dedicated to confounding the plans of those given to commodifying nature, from dambuilders to subdividers, was named George Hayduke, and he was modeled on Peacock.

Hayduke became famous. All over the West, in the men's rooms, written on walls amid the various scatologies, you'd find *Hayduke lives.* Which was most of what I knew about Peacock—*Hayduke lives.*

What to say about the rest of that night? Abbey was tall, laconic, decent, profoundly ironic, and thoughtful. He was someone I watched, the acerbic celebrity with a handsome woman at his side. I studied Abbey because I was trying to understand how to handle myself as a writer and he was a model who turned out to be funny and ironic and not an acerbic celebrity. Most of all he was dedicated, another man willing to give over his life to what he loved. But what was that? My answers are freedom, vitality, openness, willingness—juices flowing in a country where things are obviously not what they are and visible except for the thousands of shared secrets. But that's an abstract mouthful of the sort Abbey regarded as ridiculous. His opinions tended to focus on the specific. A thing I recall from that night in the Belton Chalet bar is Abbey on hydroelectric dams. "If citizens want power," he said, "tell them to shut off their goddamned lights." He could also get on your ass. At one point he eyed me and said, (I hear his old ghost now), whispering, "Did you ever try to write something you couldn't take to the prom?"

Peacock turned out to be rapid, insistent, a man so driven by his force of will and physical strength you might think he was of some other species, like, say, as some wags have said, the grizzly bear. But also, Doug was a fellow whose insights I came to value; he talked about Vietnam, working as a Green Beret medic. The killing and bloodiness, he said, made him crazy, as enough of it would make most of us crazy. He came home to find himself in a tent in the Wind River Range of Wyoming. A great black grizzly shared that territory; repeated sightings of that animal's dignity brought him back from craziness. I took Peacock to be talking about consequence. Things matter.

He said something to the effect that we can't remake the whole world in our own image or we won't have a damned thing but a world made in our own image, and that would be unworkably simple and partways dead. He said humans have to learn humility, and make allowance for otherness. We can kill everything which threatens us, we can defoliate all the jungles, but then we'd be alone. We can't kill every cat who might come to live in our night. Firepower won't save us. Humility might.

What we ought to do, he said, think of it as an exercise in learning humility, of staying in touch with what we actually are, an animal like any other, making do, is preserve a lot of territory for wilderness and creatures like the grizzly. It was a big-talking night there in the Belton Chalet. I went home and told Annick I'd made some lifetime friends.

But I didn't really know how much of his line I'd bought until the next summer, when Peacock took Annick and me to a stifling hot tent-shaped room on the second floor of an A-frame near the entrance to West Glacier, and showed us his bear films—grizzlies eyeing Peacock and his camera from fifteen feet, bears in dark-water tarns in the high country of Glacier, at play and splashing like children, running as they so famously can, with stunning agility and speed, a hundred yards in thirty seconds, over cross-drifted tangles of downed timber.

Fascinated by the insane risks involved in filming so intimately, I envied Peacock's sense of purpose, his agenda, the fact that he woke up every morning, as a friend said, with his tools still in the tunnel. Peacock and Abbey were strengthened by their convictions, inclined to act out deep beliefs and let the devil pick up the pieces. I remembered eyeing a long-ago Gila monster, and gray whales surfacing beside an aluminum boat in the Golfo de California, and found that I was two people.

One fellow was at ease in his life, settled in his prejudices. The other yearned to confidently name what he took to be sacred, and for large purposes. He was convinced the world ought to reinvent its political and economic contrivances, but to what point?

One simple autobiographical thing became clear. As a child I rode intelligent horses named Moon and Snip and watched mallards and pintails and Canada geese flying north in rafts, one above the other, calling on a spring morning. This simple thing: Early in life I'd learned to revere nature, but I hadn't acknowledged that fact in decades.

When my one-or-two-in-a-hundred-years pal, Jim Crumley, who was teaching at the University of Texas–El Paso in 1982, invited me down to give a reading in February, I concocted the idea of spending the spring in the Southwest. I was sick of gray Montana skies and busting my ass on icy sidewalks, and I had landed a yearlong sabbatical with half-time pay from the University of Montana, so why not?

Annick and I watched the Super Bowl in the bar of a Holiday Inn in Farmington, New Mexico, and then went off into light snow in the early evening. By dark the snow had turned into a blizzard. We were lucky to make the high desert town of Cuba, New Mexico. Even long-haul truckers were getting off the road. We got the last room in a sixth-rate motel with duck tape over the holes where some client had kicked in the door.

William Eastlake lived for years in the hills outside Cuba, on what he called a starve-to-death ranch. It was there he wrote the novel called *Portrait of an Artist With Twenty-Six Horses*. It's both comically surrealist and as close to what I take to be Navajo sensibilities as anything written by anybody. An old man, preparing to die, says, "There is prosperity, joy and wit and wisdom in Navajo heaven." I like to imagine Eastlake solacing himself with thoughts like that in the hills outside Cuba.

But maybe I don't understand Navajo sensibilities. An attempt to reproduce the mind-set of another culture may doom writers to what anthropologist Clifford Geertz has called "at best fiction." Or it may be that Eastlake got it dead right. Maybe his New Mexico novels are masterworks, and prime to be rediscovered. Let's hope so.

Eastlake said Cuba was ultimately too isolated, and Navajo sensibilities, however much he admired them, were not his. They were way too far out-of-the-mainstream for a man who'd grown up in New Jersey and studied for years in Europe. Cuba, he said, drove him to dreams of breaking glass and wildness. Too much nowhere to go but out for the mail, too much distance and not enough spice of life. Too much grasping at straws.

When I met him, in southeastern Oregon during the summer of 1969, Eastlake was theoretically teaching a two-week writing workshop in Bend. But he drifted away after only a few days. I don't know that he returned. We went to Crater Lake, and he squinted and said, imitating some movie director he'd come to loath, "Scrub the island."

The next weekend we were in Eugene. Eastlake called the late, lamented Ken Kesey. He said they were pals. At Kesey's house (the famous painted bus sat in a shed beside the barn) we lost track and then it was morning and I was somehow awake in a bed in the house where I belonged in Eugene. I didn't see Eastlake again for more than a decade.

Daylight in Cuba came up bright and windless and vividly cold, but we were on a warm patio in Santa Fe for lunch. Annick and I rented a casita uphill from the square, and after an evening nap we ambled into a dark dining room and sat before a fire and made a late meal on famous snacks—smoked salmon, Guaymas shrimp, hot brie with lingonberries, and the tentacles of deep-fried squid.

We woke to the melting snow of another nighttime storm, and laziness. It was a day to lay up and forego agendas. A book to travel with is Czeslaw Milosz: "The smell of winter apples, of hoarfrost, and of linen. There are nothing but gifts on this poor, poor earth."

In El Paso, Jim Crumley hustled us across the bridge into the chaos of downtown Juárez, where we stood up at the bar in the famous Kentucky Club (colonized by United States military men from Kentucky during World War I). A white ceramic tile-work urinal ran the foot of the bar, and Annick was delighted to witness an old man calmly pissing into it. This, again, was it. Any sweet striking thing could happen.

What did happen was unshucked oysters. Crumley persuaded a friend to bring a barley sack filled with hundreds of oysters back from a trip to Corpus Christi, and threw what seemed to be a forever-and-ever party for a crowd of his assorted writer and biker cronies. I still bear a scar on my left thumb from a moment of awkwardness while trying to shuck one of those oysters. We never did eat them all. But it was a failure we loved, born of plenitude and generosity.

Driving along the El Paso side of the Rio Grande we could see over into the profound back-street poverties of Juárez— mile after mile of adobe houses with tacked-on rooms of scrap lumber and cardboard, roofed with tar paper and patched with flattened tin cans. No tree or greenery in sight along unpaved, dusty streets. Isolated men and women walked slowly toward no goal we could make out. "What do those people do?" Annick asked. "All day job just surviving," Crumley said.

It's semi-impossible for people like me, from the privileged end of things, to grasp what's going on in a town like Juárez. What I realize is the degree that I'm insulated from the feelings of people who labor so mightily just to sustain hope. I'm incapable, because of my background, of even seeing much of what's there, or who's there, what they're doing. I don't know how to see it, or them. Even so, those injustices I have trouble seeing are to a great degree my responsibility.

Two problems are waiting to explode in the Southwest. The first centers on injustices along the border, the other is aridity, ecological fragility. Cities like Phoenix and Tucson and Albuquerque are booming—too many people, a huge number of them poor, and there is not enough water. So, thirst, both actual and metaphoric.

Crumley took me on an all-day road trip along the Mexico/New Mexico border, to visit a fellow he knew in the tiny community of Columbus, New Mexico, where Pancho Villa invaded the

United States only to be defeated by forces under the command of Gen. Black Jack Pershing, later an American leader during World War I in France.

Our first move was into a tavern, this one in the town of Palomas on the Mexican side of the border where I paid for a round of tequila with a twenty-dollar bill and was startled when a man came from a back room, snatched it up, and vanished out the door. We were into a second go-round on the tequila before he returned in triumph, clutching a handful of greenbacks. He'd been up and down both sides of the street finding change for my twenty.

Money wasn't a problem on the United States side of the border. Crumley's friend lived in one of a long string of well-kept houses along the highway north into New Mexico, where he was storing the remnants of a defunct Pancho Villa museum. This subdivision was only one-house deep, backed up to an airstrip. Most householders had an airplane.

Escape and freedom were strong considerations in this community of the like-minded. The people who lived there were concerned that the poor and people of color, led by communists, might rise up and begin taking over the civilized world. There in the shimmering isolation of Columbus, New Mexico, they were hidden. Their larders were stocked, their aircraft fueled. They were ready to fly out.

Where they planned to go I have no idea. Maybe to the mythic distances of backland Paraguay. Maybe they owned ranches down there. Maybe airstrips and servants were waiting patiently in Paraguay. But probably not. These were not the very rich but rather the huddled, dithering well-to-do, people who had learned to tell themselves a story about flying away in order to survive the end of industrial civilization and white-man privilege as it presently exists.

It would be too easy to write off that cluster hiding out in Columbus, New Mexico, as lunatics. They were only trying to care for themselves. Dislocation and dangers we think we see lurking in the world drive lots of people, including me, some of the time, quite frantic.

Nevertheless, they were armed, thus dangerous in my eyes. What I wanted most fervently was distance between me and what I saw as paranoid-unto-craziness loonies. Maybe I was as fright-ened as they were. In any event, soon we were gone, in El Paso by nightfall and back to playing bulletproof, shucking more oysters.

What is it with desert rats, reprobates, anarchic adventurers, profoundly conservative runaways? Wandering the semi-postmodern wonderland of the "new Southwest," I keep in mind the greathearted but profoundly ironic spirit of Ed Abbey.

At the end of *Desert Solitaire* Abbey says, "I am a desert rat. But why? And why, in precisely what way, is the desert more alluring, more baffling, more fascinating than either the moun-tains or the sea?"

Trying to answer himself, Abbey writes, "The desert says nothing. Completely passive, acted upon but never acting, the desert lies there like the bare skeleton of Being, spare, sparse, austere, utterly worthless, inviting not love but contemplation.

"The desert waits outside, desolate and still and strange, unfamiliar and often grotesque in its forms and colors, inhabited by rare, furtive creatures of incredible hardiness and cunning, colonized by weird mutants from the plant kingdom, most of them spiny, thorny, stunted, and twisted as they are tenacious."

Then an operative line: "There is something about the desert that the human sensibility cannot assimilate."

And, "Behind the dust, meanwhile under the vulture-haunted sky, the desert waits, mesa, butte, canyon, reef, sink, escarpment, pinnacle, maze, dry lake, sand dune and barren mountain—untouched by the human mind."

So, untouchable. Going to the desert, Abbey seems to be telling us, is sort of like going to the stars, to a weave of energies that cannot be transmogrified. Sort of like dying, our fragile and frightened individualism subsumed into the labyrinth of everything.

So what's the attraction? Maybe clarity, clear air, seeing over distances. The desert doesn't conceal or bother to lie. The stories we hide behind don't play well against a long backdrop of timelessness. Maybe a chance at life seen clearly, joys and sorrows of birth, sex, and senescence, and that ultimate question "What then?" taken straight because there's no other option.

Speculation about the early Christian monks who retreated to the Egyptian desert—the Desert Fathers—tends to center on the notion of renunciation and consequent chances at spiritual clarity. Maybe that's part of it, tipping your hat and saying a compromised good-bye to desire so as to get on with the real business of life. Which is what? Maybe Keats was right—he said soulmaking.

Ultimately the Southwest is dry territory. Aridity places a nearly absolute limit on the possibilities of life there.

Too many people, not enough water, one hundred or more days with temperatures over 100 degrees, too many automobiles and too much air-conditioning, too many human fantasies heedlessly acted out, endless misuse of the land and people. That's the beginning of a common litany of complaints about the contemporary Southwest.

The pristine clarity of dry air over the deserts has been taken to be a natural metaphor for clearly defined purposes, and it is increasingly murky. Haze from the power plant at Page hangs in the Grand Canyon. The skies over Phoenix are ordinarily obscured by a dull dun-colored smog. Treasures like the glory of Glen Canyon are drowned.

As the wreckage is accepted as normal, chances of utter Mad Max–land ruin are incrementally closer. The ghost of Edward Abbey tells me to say things like that, to demand a responsible and itemized adding up of the actual human and biological costs of "progress," to resist the downtown forces of commodification while insisting on the absolute value of every enfranchised and disenfranchised being, from the tiny bats helping to pollinate cactus as they feed at blossoms in the night to the men raging away their lives in the reeking dungeons under cell blocks in Florence Prison. Every being.

Like so many solitaries, Abbey was an outlander who learned to value silences. His ghost is with me as I write this book. I imagine Ed Abbey shaking his head at my pontificating, muttering, laughing, popping a top. The old black-and-silver magpie man.

After our time in El Paso with Jim Crumley, Annick and I drove to Tucson, and Doug Peacock led us out back of his house near the junction between Silver Bell and Ina Road, and showed us flowering. The relationship between insects and cactus and bats, nighttime insemination and blossoming, was actually interesting not to speak of sacred.

Deserts, to a fellow like me, who grew up in the highland sagebrush country of the Great Basin, meant arid, gray, a simple ecology which never blossomed (never mind that it's not true in the Great Basin, that I stomped on desert wildflowers all the years of my upbringing without really seeing them because my society had taught me to believe flowers were of no consequence). Desert meant arid wasteland, no blossoming.

Prepared to be bored, I followed Annick and Peacock off into semi-urban remnants of desert, into arroyos with houses on nearby ridges. I found that the Sonoran Desert ecology was as complex as that of a rain forest.

There's one workable way to know any environment and that's get intimate, slow down and meander, touch, smell and see, respond. Spring on the Sonoran Desert played in us, after a few hours of goofing around in the arroyos, like Mozart.

There are, their characteristics determined by elevation, a stack of "life zones," biological systems, in the island mountain ranges of the Southwest. The commonly accepted idea of life zones was developed almost a century ago by Dr. C. Hart Merriam after a biological survey of the San Francisco Mountain peaks near Flagstaff. Ascending from the alluvial plains and creosote playas in extreme lowlands involves working through transitions, changes in adapted animal and plant species, to the Arctic–Alpine Zone above 11,500 feet, where pika and mountain sheep live amid mosses and rocks.

At the top of the Santa Catalina Mountains behind Tucson there are yellow-pine forests like those in the northern Rockies. Lower down creeks fall through canyons which constitute flowering enclaves where hummingbirds and butterflies inhabit a springtime paradise. People ski above Tucson, only a few miles from others who are rubbing on sunblock before heading out to hike among the saguaro cactus, while others are testing their touch on greens that run to a speed of eleven on the Stimpmeter at 150-dollar-a-round golf resorts.

Peacock simply led us out to wander behind his house. We were in the desert where people most like to live—the *bajada*—stony uplands rising from the flats, where the mix of plant and animal species is most various, where the trophy houses cluster.

The truly posh neighborhoods are on the bajada. Annick and I recently lived a couple of weeks in a friend's house just where the bajada lifts into the wilderness of the Santa Catalinas. We saw January snow on saguaro outside the back door. In Phoenix the wealthy cluster below Camelback Mountain and, to the north, in Carefree, and out around the Nicklaus complex of golf courses at Desert Mountain (more bajada).

From the bajada, from a patio on a ridge top, you can gaze down on the lighted flatlands of Tucson at night. Our species once found safety from attack by hunting cats through living on ledges, backs to the wall, where they could see out over the hunting grounds. A preference for this kind of setting was built into our nervous systems as the generations evolved. So, the well-to-do enjoy looking down on the less fortunate. It helps them feel invulnerable. Which we all yearn to do.

Doug ambled, naming and explaining. Flowering cactuses and wildflowers blossom spectacularly in the bajada—bloody red, golden, white, purple. Ocotillo flowers red, tiny flowers; it's called coachman's whip, and instantly sprouts new leaves after a rain. The creosote brush has varnish on its leaves to seal in moisture, and releases its perfume in late July when the monsoon rains fall on the desert at night. Doug showed us the nests built by cactus wrens in behind the spines of the cholla; their nests, called pouches, where their young stay cool and humidified, sealed inside the woven layers of dry grass and feathers. He told us to watch out for the jumping cholla. One spine in your forearm, give a twitch, and there it is, an entire little limb of the cholla hanging from your flesh.

This kind of information came at us frenetically, Peacock babbling, a man eager to talk about photosynthesis in stems, naming the little cactuses, the barrel and the prickly pear, both of which flower bright yellow in April, and the foothill paloverde, which also flowers yellow in April.

"Mexican poppies, you ought to see it." So we did, one afternoon we drove north on the freeway toward Phoenix, and hiked through wildnesses thick with tangerine-orange flowers, a splendor defying all but the most intractable despair.

It's an Arizona custom to go seeking wildflowers in spring. The blossoming is most spectacular after a rainy winter. Devotees count more than forty species—up to eighty—in a single day: indigo, delphinium, desert and Coulter's hibiscus, tackstem and penstemon, fairy duster, desert onion, and on and on, name your favorites.

Others chase hummingbirds in their flittering, the red-throated and the calliope, and ruby-crowned kinglets. Or they pursue flocks of sandhill cranes moving north to the tundras, snowy egrets and blue-throated hummingbirds and turkey vultures arriving for the summer. Osprey and rufous hummingbirds are just passing through. Hummingbirds, I can't stop listing them, move me to my fanciest fantasies. The white-eared and the magnificent, so many species in flowering havens all day long, so intricate in their speedy doings, so elegant in their comings and goings, such quick splendor.

The emblematic life form of the bajada is the saguaro. It germinates from black seeds so infinitesimally tiny, they're best seen under a magnifying glass; and so tough, they can lie dormant for fifteen years and still come awake.

The saguaro grows very slowly at first, maybe seven inches in ten years, and only branches when it reaches a height of ten feet. Mature saguaro have been recorded at fifty feet in height, with over fifty arms. The skin is smooth, another cactus with a waxy coating to prevent water loss. Under the skin, over a cylinder of wooden rods which reinforces the external ribs, is a layer of pulpy tissue which expands when water is absorbed. The body of the cactus, where Gila woodpeckers and gilded flickers tunnel and build self-healing nests in the flesh, thus forms a water storage tower, which roots itself most securely in shallow rocky soil like that of the bajada.

The saguaro blooms in spring, at night, a flowering which is white in color, with dense yellow stamens in a deep tube where sweet nectar accumulates. Moths and other insects and two species of bats go from flower to flower, pollinating, and soon fruit begins to form, each with four thousand seeds and as large as a hen's egg. When ripe, the fruit split, revealing the bright red insides which are often mistaken for a flower. Birds take this fruit, seeds are scattered. The old symbolic giant reproduces.

Part of the pleasure in witnessing this resulted from coming to understand that processes of this kind are going on everywhere. It was for me, once a farmer who believed that ecologies could be manipulated in simple one-off ways, a door opening on the constantly evolving interwoven complexities of where we are. And, thus, what we are. But no info on why.

Recently, in *High Country News,* Craig Childs wrote of hiking the beds of streams coming out of the Galiuro Mountains northeast of Phoenix, in high summer. The daytime temperatures were around 120 degrees. Too hot for the snakes. In summer, water in the streams percolates up from underground, but some dry up during the daytime as root systems of trees and brush along the stream bed suck up all the water. Then the night cools, the trees and brush don't need to absorb so much water to survive, and streams flow again. The most amazing thing, to the non-biologist, are the tiny fish that have evolved to survive in those streams. They get through the hot summer by spending long hours of daylight torpor in sponges of soaked algae under leaf piles or in rotten wood. Then, when the water flows, they reemerge. Water beetles, which survive in the same way, also emerge, and fireflies. By late evening the stream is alive again. This sort of thing has been going on for thousands and thousands of years, adapting and evolving. The Galiuro Mountains, far off on an eastern horizon, looked to be a never-never land—no roads on the maps I had. We never went there. A good thing that was.

Craig Childs also tells of tiny fish that live in a pool fed by springs high on a terrace above the Grand Canyon. Their ancestors inhabited that landlocked pool for the millions of years it took the Colorado Plateau to rise and for the river to cut the canyon down through it. Thank God he doesn't give an exact location. Those natural systems are, in their delicate intricacy, invaluable, and don't need the likes of me and you stomping around.

Driving back to Peacock's house, hungry and ready to sniff the gin bottle, we were startled when a herd of javelina, wild desert pigs, crossed the road. "They're habituated," Doug said. "Next thing, they'll be turning over garbage cans in the night."

Annick flew back to Montana, and Peacock and Ed Abbey and I drove down to visit Bill Eastlake in Naco, which overlooks the Mexican border south of Bisbee, where Eastlake had settled to make his last stand. We played a hour or so of half-wit pool at a table Eastlake had in what seemed to be a "family room," then went off for steaks and conviviality at the Copper Queen Hotel in Bisbee. Eastlake had aged seriously, and was no longer the fellow I'd last seen in Ken Kesey's barn. There we are, in memory, posed as if for picture-taking out front of the old Copper Queen Hotel, pretending we're barricaded against frailties, and now we're otherwise.

"All I wanted," Eastlake said, "was to get published in a literary magazine. Then a first-rate literary magazine, then a slick-paper national magazine, then a novel, then a well-reviewed novel, then a well-reviewed novel that sold hundreds of thousands of copies, a book everybody was talking about. Made it most of the way but never took that last step." He laughed.

Eastlake was telling us the heart was gone from his life, not because he'd never gotten rich and famous but because the ambitions that drove him to stay with it through a lifetime of work were dead. He wasn't telling us that his ambitions had been foolish, just that they were over, and so was he. I never saw him again after shaking his hand good-bye on the porch of the Copper Queen Hotel in Bisbee.

CHAPTER THREE

Homelands

Going south, Annick and I look forward to entering a country where the place-names sing like music—Zuni and Hopi and Navajo, Apache, pueblo and Chicano names, Penitente names: Acoma, Truchas, Kaibito, Jicarilla, Aramosa, Shonto, Betatakin, Kayenta, Chilchinbito, Shungopavi, Sipaulovi, Oraibi, Laguna, Taos, Santa Fe, Jemez, Cochiti. And El Paso, Albuquerque, Tucson, Phoenix.

Why does this run of place-names sound so like music? Partways because they're musical, but maybe more so because I tend to think of the people and cultures who live in conjunction to those places as examples of accomplished ways to live, and because some of those cultures have proven to be enduring.

Most of us spend a lot of energy telling ourselves a story in which our homeland is defined and located. Homelands are specific, but their qualities have to do with much more than landforms.

The most secure home, we know from history and our experience, is in the coherent self, but it's also comforting to feel physically located. Where you know how water should taste, where the migrating birds arrive on time, and landforms personify stories about geologic upthrusts, and you hear other stories in the barbershop, some scandalous. Where you of course know your neighbors, when and how they came, why they stayed, and whether or not their children who went off to law school and/or drugs in the cities will ever return.

Apache on the White Mountain Apache Reservation in eastern Arizona, according to anthropologist Keith Basso, in *Wisdom Sits in Places,* name the physical particularities of their territory—river crossings and rocky outcroppings—after incidents that took place nearby, like "Widows Pause for Breath" or "She Carries Her Brother on Her Back." The Apache live not only in places but in a webwork of names which imply stories about who they are, moral stories about the consequences of foolishness and the rewards of generosity, about acting right, about decency and forgiveness, or, as Basso says, "morality, politeness and tact."

In *Zuni and the American Imagination*, Eliza McFeely says the people at Zuni pueblo balance "cultural independence against the steady pressure of America's mass-produced homogeneity." The Zuni exists simultaneously as community and tourist attraction, but a semi-timeless Zuni can still be found, "an archaeological treasure buried beneath new buildings, hidden around the corners of the treacherously winding roads, quietly playing second fiddle to the beckoning marquee of the video store."

Homelands are, simply enough, emotional homes. Beyond that they can be defined in many ways. The Southwest is a weave, from Mexican-American neighborhoods on the south side of Tucson to pueblos along the Rio Grande to the designer environs of Santa Fe, from upscale Scottsdale to isolated Navajo hogans, from Sun City after Sun City, from Acoma pueblo to the cotton farms south of Phoenix, from survivalists in the highlands of New Mexico to seekers after divine crystal wisdom in Sedona. The Southwest is itself a homeland, the Hopi pueblos are homelands, and middle-class neighborhoods in Phoenix are homelands. They can be as large as our nation or small as the valley where I grew up, large as the Colorado River watershed, small as a village or rural family. We usually live in more than one at a time; they nest inside one another. I remember a litany from when I was a child: "me, our house, school, Adel, Lake County, Oregon, U.S.A., North America, the world, the universe." I used to write it in my schoolbooks. In the Southwest, ancient homelands tend to cluster where by accidents of nature there was water to sustain crops like corn and squash, places like Zuni and the pueblos along the Rio Grande. And there are newcomer homelands, Mormon communities, mining towns like Globe or Bisbee, and retirement towns like Green Valley. Each can be a position from which to enjoy and withstand the gorgeous, evasive, and invasive world, or to despair.

In 1932, at Blackwater Draw, near the New Mexico/Texas border on the Llano Estacato ("staked plain"), the most extensive flatland on earth, a highway crew came up with a precisely worked stone knife in conjunction with a huge animal tooth. Blackwater Draw turned out to be a Pleistocene oasis, where shallow ponds drew mammals and their human hunters.

Archaeologists flocked in, did their digging, and established that men (the Clovis culture) had hunted mammoths, camels, bison, horses, turtles, and small animals near the ponds along Blackwater Draw from very roughly 11,500 to 10,900 B.P. (before present). The Clovis people were followed by a culture of large-game hunters called the Folsom complex, known to have the best weaponry in the world for that time.

Through these centuries North America suffered one of the world's severest episodes of species die-out. Herbivores, from twenty-foot ground sloths to beaver the size of bears, together with horses, camels, mastadons, and musk oxen, vanished and were soon followed into extinction by carnivores who lived off them, lions and cheetahs, saber-toothed cats, the dire wolf and the short-faced bear—twice the size of our grizzly.

While human hunting beyond doubt contributed to the die-out—a theory called the Overkill Hypothosis—a long period of global warming (the water table hasn't reached the surface at Blackwater Draw in the past five thousand years) had more to do with it. Human hunters moved on to other ways of life.

We aren't much different in our psychic capabilities from early men, and we too are involved in overkill and global warming. Can we learn from their example? Sure. The theorizing goes this way: Everything evolves. Nothing lasts. Don't destroy that which your people depend on. Take care, and plan for the seventh generation, the long future.

The Southwest is as populated, given environmental realities, as it reasonably can be (urban areas are vastly *over*populated), and the people who last tend to be tough-minded. In *Pueblo: Mountain, Village, Dance,* the preeminent architectural scholar, Vincent Scully, Jr., says the ancient people, as their country dried up and they were forced to move from homelands where they had invested enormous efforts over hundreds of years, were held together by their "most important possession: the incomparably rich and intricate structure of their ceremonial lives." Scully calls native peoples in the Southwest "American empiricists, hopeful, reasonable, and hard. Something true and clear, massively unsentimental, runs through all their works."

The native cultures are stoic, ironic, mystic, and practical, dreaming, praying, whimsical empiricists. Their lands are populated by stories about those who came before, beings who they often called ghosts. Even newcomers like Abbey might be counted among the ghosts.

After the demise of the great mammals, people wandered the deserts and canyons, hunting creatures they could find and gathering seeds and nuts, cactus fruits and various greens. Following a three-thousand-year drought, people returned to the Southwest about 2,500 years ago and settled in watered places so as to pursue small-scale farming. Maize and squash, cultivated crops vital to the civilizations of central Mexico, made their way north 1,500 years ago (many plants in the Southwest were harvested for food but none were domesticated).

People dug pit houses four to six feet into the earth, and roofed them with beams. A house took some three to four hundred hours of labor to construct. People began living in villages and producing well-made sandals and cradleboards.

People lived longer, had more children, and more of their children survived; populations increased. Settled life was easier on the aged, and women in villages were able to reproduce more often than those wandering in search of food. By A.D. 500 pottery, hard for wanderers to transport because of its weight and fragility, was in common use. For thousands of years food had been communally owned. Rules for sharing were clearly defined. But now each household had its private stores, its wealth. Class distinctions evolved, and divisions of labor, elites, even work gangs.

Common rooms and buildings used for religious purposes, eventually kivas, were being constructed. Communities and religious leaders were increasingly focused on directing and placating the forces and spirits they believed to be in control of their world. Farmers have always been vitally interested in predicting weather, frosts and rainfall, the seasons. Complex astrological observations, over decades, centuries, eventually became a cultural obsession. Shamans, in their trances, sent their spirits out into time and space, searching for information, messages.

But most important, for the eventual development of civilization, there was trade with Mesoamerica, in turquoise and tropical feathers, musical instruments like conch-shell trumpets, copper bells—and food. High cultures in the Southwest were on the frontier, extensions of elaborate civilizations in Mesoamerica. Beans from Mexico provided complex amino acids missing in maize and squash, and contributed to healthier diets. Ideas and goods came north along many routes, predominantly by way of the largest settlement in the prehistoric Southwest, Casas Grande in what is now Chihuahua, Mexico, a pueblo with finally more than two thousand rooms. There, macaws for trade were bred in captivity.

The obviously related religions practiced in the native Southwest today also seem to have evolved from beliefs come north from Mesoamerica. Which doesn't mean that native cultures in the Southwest should be thought of as derivative. Their beliefs seem to be, rather, a morally sensible flowering of ancient ideas.

Regional traditions evolved. While language studies suggest a much wider diversity, prehistoric cultures identified by scholars as distinct are the Hohokam, Mogollon, and Anasazi.

In the Navajo language, Anasazi is sometimes taken to mean "ancient enemies." It's a usage not favored by native peoples, seen as dismissive and/or divisive. "Ancient Pueblo Ancestors" or "Desert Archaic Peoples" are politically correct ways to go. But I'll keep saying Anasazi, a word that sings of my yearning to know what it was like to have been alive at Chaco Canyon. I apologize but there I am. There was, after all, warfare among tribes. Why pretend otherwise?

In any event, at the rim of the Grand Canyon and in the deserts of southern Utah, having reached the ecological limit of a corn economy, those cultures went no farther.

The Hohokam—"those who are gone" to the O'odham, who are likely their descendants—lived in villages and farmed along the Salt, Pima, and Verde Rivers of what's now Arizona.

Their culture is famous for a hand-excavated irrigation system—diversion weirs in the rivers, canals extending ten to fifteen miles from the river, head gates paved with stones. The Lehi canal system, fed by the Salt River near the modern city of Mesa, Arizona, leads to Mesa Grande, a great house atop the largest platform mound in the the Hohokam territory, and a cultural center for as many as sixty thousand people in the Phoenix Basin by the late thirteenth century. This was certainly the greatest density of population anywhere in the prehistoric Southwest. As well as corn, beans, and squash, they grew cotton, agave, and other native plants. Village ball courts, of which there were 225, imply a ritual system for healing the community together, resolving animosities.

As a boy I herded water down garden ditches between rows of strawberries, corn, and squash. As a young man I farmed three thousand acres of alfalfa and domesticated grasses, and another three thousand acres of barley on irrigated land in the high-desert country of southeastern Oregon. Water rushed into fields, bringing life to life. My purposes ran with the flowing.

So I love maps which outlined traces of the Hohokam irrigation systems. This I understand. But the Hohokam archaeological sites lie on a dusty flatland, and are a not-much-to-see cultural phenomena. So I thought. I could have imagined ancient lives, birds and water murmuring like acquaintances. Maybe whoever it was there, south of the Salt River a thousand years ago, found themselves, as I had in southeastern Oregon, happy at the thought of getting in on the greening up, irrigating and thus triggering fecundity. I could have loved the notion that Hohokam irrigators and I are versions of the same old confounded creature. But I didn't, I was focused on other continuities. Phoenix was vibrating along as usual, and I was hot to make a spring-training game in Scottsdale, and then retire to the casual upscale ambiance of Pischke's Paradise, a tavern where the chic byword is "No Sniveling."

The Mogollon lived in the piney mountains and grassland valleys of east-central Arizona and west-central New Mexico, a cooler, wetter, sometimes snowy country. These days it's given over to mining centers like Silver City, hideaway cattle ranches, hunting camps, and towns like Pinetop, where people from the shimmeringly lowlands gather on summer weekends to cool off.

The Mogollon hunted, gathered piñon nuts, juniper berries, walnuts, and cactus fruits, and cultivated, without irrigation, maize, squash, and beans. They built pit houses, and eventually moved to above-ground sets of rooms comparable to modern pueblos. Many tribal groups in the Southwest believe life flows between this apparent world and various underworlds, and stage ceremonies in underground shrines called kivas. The Mogollon were in on the beginning of this tradition.

To me the most interesting of the Mogollon lived along the Rio Mimbres in southwestern New Mexico. Around A.D. 1000-1150, within a generation, they developed a style of decorating ceramic bowls—mostly black images around a curving white interior—which is as imaginatively valuable as any produced by people anywhere. But the bowls were not art objects. As is shown by wear patterns, they were in household use. As bowls.

The images inside those bowls, however, of both common and mythic figures, sometimes with simultaneous human and animal characteristics, images of sacrifice and beheading, and of figures which resemble the kachinas of contemporary pueblo religion, seem to have been of ritual significance. Most of the existing bowls were recovered from graves (often by pot hunters, to sell on an upscale international market, a swinish, devious practice which continues). The Mogollon Mimbres wrapped the dead in cloth, positioned the body in a pit alongside a wall, then covered the head with an inverted bowl with a small hole punched in the bottom (the bowl was said to have been "killed" or sacrificed). What was allowed to escape, the soul, excessive grief, or perhaps seriousness?

I say seriousness because those bowls, commonplace and sacred in Mimbres houses, reek both of dignity and whimsy (that sacred combination). As a friend said, "They remind us of what life is." She meant, I think, the joke, the tragedy, salt and sweetness, to be enjoyed, and forever lost. The often profoundly ironic, cool-hearted, dualistic, and geometric images were likely the work of women (stunning art produced by a few generations in economically marginal villages, the artists all known to one another) who traditionally shaped and fired pottery. The tails of identifiable animals intertwine and lead off into a circle of sine waves. What are we supposed to see here, animals or the cosmos? Or that things large and small are irrevocably interwoven and at play with one another?

The images likely refer to concepts of sacred space and cosmic geography still commonly accepted in pueblo cultures. Homelands and community are understood to be at a "central place," which was sought for and found by their ancestors, a space both metaphoric and physical, framed by mountains, springs, caves, and shrines. The Mimbres bowls are circum-scribed by a framing line around the rim, and may have been thought of as both a map of and prayer for an orderly, bounded world, safe and fertile, however complex.

Cryptic and elegantly drawn, often beyond our powers of interpretation, illusional, the images refer to the everyday and myth in a constant dancing—with counter rhythms and multi-ple symmetries, evolving, never to make as much sense as we'd like and yet to be revered. Domesticated space inside a house-hold bowl. Mimbres women, in their obscure valley, would have been ideal illustrators for work by Borges and Nabokov.

As with the Hohokam irrigators, I have to think their lives were ultimately like ours. Their responses are enduring-ly, profoundly instructive and useful, even reassuring. They saw as we do, and their example helps me accept the limita-tions of what I am and lead me to wonder what we mean by progress? Toward what?

Populations exploded in the Southwest after a period of above-average rainfall around A.D. 1000, increasing ten- to twenty-fold. The people of the deserts, the Anasazi, spread and filtered to the bottom of the Grand Canyon and to the tops of isolated buttes.

At Chaco Canyon they began work on nine "great houses." As Annick and I walked the ruins there under a blazing sky, fingering the intricately stacked stony balustrades of Pueblo Bonito, we were spooky, uneasy. Perhaps because windy, echo-ing silences and emptiness carried news about the fragility of our lives and families and downtowns and yearnings, colored by the elegance of those remains. All this, and it was not enough?

The great houses were built during a brief florescence in Chaco between A.D. 1025 and A.D. 1100—an enormous project. It's conjectured that great houses were headquarters for a theocracy ruling an area "only slightly smaller than Ireland." This is reinforced by the fact that while only two thousand people seem to have lived full time at Chaco, there was space for some five thousand. Perhaps Chaco Canyon was a ceremonial center and central marketplace, always prepared for an influx of pilgrims and traders.

Native architecture from Chaco to Zuni and Acoma and Hopi to the Rio Grande pueblos imitates desert landforms, mesas, and rimrocks. Vincent Scully, Jr., in *Pueblo: Mountain, Village, Dance* says such structures were almost works of nature, like "the homes of bees." But Chaco seems to have been a devised rather than evolved community, intensively planned and precisely built by a large managed work force. The houses were fitted together from tons of red stone cut in quarries and mortared into tapered load-bearing walls, five stories high on the curving back side of the Pueblo Bonito. Tens of thousands of pine timbers were cut and trimmed with stone axes in mountains sixty miles away and brought to Chaco by people without horses or wheels. Generations labored away for many thousands of hours fashioning the constructions along the wash in Chaco Canyon.

What drove them to such efforts? Force, or belief? I sensed the ghosts of slave/master relationships, and repression. But maybe I had Chaco wrong. Maybe the people who lived there built to honor the solace and power given to them by a spiritual idea. Exacting work, doors and windows absolutely aligned as at Chaco, each stone precisely and particularly fitted—is not often produced on demand. Maybe Chaco should be thought as made sacred by generations of devotion, like Chartres or Machu Picchu. I'm reminded of utterly joined Inca walls. On the other hand, in his long poem, *The Heights of Machu Picchu,* Neruda decried what he thought of as the slavery involved in that labor.

As Vincent Scully, Jr., says, the pueblos were built to support a ceremonial system dedicated to influencing the gods of the natural world, essentially, to bring rain. They are most fundamentally a setting for prayer and ceremony.

The world view of the people at Chaco, according to archaeologist Stephen H. Lekson, is based on "myths concerning the emergence of people from the earth in the time of genesis and their subsequent migration to a place of settlement." This shows in "the correspondence between man-made symbolic constructions and abstract notions of cosmic geometry." The "architectural and ritual repetition of these themes established immutable points of reference and order."

People from Chaco cleared long straight roads with staircases cut into sandstone rims, thus connecting themselves to outlier villages and at the same time delineating their sacred geography, an entire landscape understood as a staging ground for ritual based on cosmology. North/south roads were likely routes along which pilgrimages progressed toward a sacred "central place" where humans lived. Chacoans kept exact track of seasons and equinoxes, serving both ceremonial and agricultural purposes. The pueblos spread over four square miles in an integrated, built, and urban environment. But not all was symbolic. They channeled rainwater off mesas to farms along the wash. Old men sat in the sun and watched young women, squash blossomed and children played in the water, laughing.

Then, around A.D. 1150, Chaco was abandoned. The people, anthropologists think, mostly went north to the San Juan River drainage, to Aztec pueblo and Mesa Verde. Some drifted west to the Hopi pueblos and south to those at Zuni.

We tend to think of preliterate peoples, around the world, as stuck in place. But that's not true. Tribes were constantly moving on to new ground, in long waves, a few miles in every generation. It's a mostly unknown history, recorded only in communal memories, stories transformed into legends and then myths.

Europeans came to North America, New England and Virginia, to the middle West, in waves. They came all the way West only generations ago, on the move, in search of homes. Which perhaps accounts for our eagerness to fathom reasons why a people so securely in place as the Anasazi in Chaco Canyon—who worked endlessly to construct elaborate homes for themselves—would abruptly take part in the "abandonments."

Across the Southwest, by A.D. 1250, culminating around A.D. 1300, there was a general depopulation of major settlements. The Mogollon had already been absorbed into the Anasazi; the Hohokam and Anasazi cultures collapsed; building construction and most craftwork ceased. There were of course causes. But no one claims to know specifically what they were.

Between A.D. 1090 and 1100, and between 1130 and 1180, there were severe droughts. It's possible that dry winters, and monsoon rains in the summer, resulted in gully washing. Chaco Wash is presently cut by a deep channel, which lowered the water table to the point that subirrigated agriculture is now impossible. In conjunction with salination in the irrigated soils, and the gradual killing off of large hunting animals, prolonged drought and the subsequent gully washing may have led to starvations.

But if that's so, why did the dispossessed tend to resettle on cliff-top mesas or in caves high on almost unclimbable cliffs? It seems they were intent on defending themselves. Against whom?

For answers to such questions, we have unsubstantiated speculation. It's been theorized they may have been terrorized by hunter-gatherer bands of the Athapascans who had come south from the Mackenzie River Delta of northwestern Canada at roughly this time. No one knows how long they had been on the move, or if they came south through the Rocky Mountains or followed bison across the short-grass plains. Confronted by what must have seemed an infinity of deserts, they began settling and interacting with the people who became the Hopi and Zuni and those in the pueblos along the Rio Grande. Their culture evolved into that of the present-day Navajo and Apache. But there's no evidence of armed conflict. Except, of course, for the name, Anasazi, sometimes taken to mean "ancient enemies."

Or, did a theocracy lose control? Did an uprising run across the deserts in reaction to colonialist overlords from the high cultures of Mesoamerica? Were the rebels fearing retribution?

This kind of guessing isn't utterly off the wall. Through neutron activation analysis, turquoise in the ancient Toltec trading system across central Mexico has been shown to have been mostly mined in the Southwest. Then there are those parrot feathers, found in Hohokam and Anasazi ruins. Clearly, there was back-and-forth contact.

By the beginning of the fourteenth century, archaeological evidence indicates that much of the Southwest, including areas which had been densely populated, were emptied of human presence. The people had moved from Chaco to Mesa Verde and to cliff houses (defensive positions) like the White House in Canyon de Chelly, Betatakin and Keet Seel in Tesgi Wash, where they stayed for a generation. Tree-ring dating shows that Betatakin, with 135 rooms and perhaps 125 residents, was only lived in from 1267 to perhaps 1300. What drove them to keep moving? We can only guess.

Arroyo Hondo, a pueblo of 1,200 two-story rooms, was built in the years between A.D. 1315 and 1330, then abandoned, then resettled in the 1370s. It was burned and abandoned again in A.D. 1410. The people ate starvation foods such as cattails, cholla, and grass seeds. Infant mortality was high— 26 percent died before the age of one, and 45 percent died before five. The average age was 16.6 years.

But other tribal people were congregating in places where they were to settle and stay, around the Hopi mesas and at Zuni and Acoma and Laguna, and in pueblos along the Rio Grande, where there was more reliable water and they were able to count on their crops. They built high-walled defensive pueblos, no doorways on the ground floor but rather ladders that could be pulled up in times of attack; they developed societies in which personal, social, and religious relationships were woven together in a complex fabric which did not easily unravel; they acted out their prayers, planted and hunted and harvested, and danced in time with what they took to be the rhythms of the cosmos.

The time of resettlement after the so-called abandonment can be thought of as one of cultural reinvention. The problems of coexistence were at least partially resolved. Commonly known stories and sacred rituals brought people into sanctified relationships and allegiances. Status was almost exclusively based on taking care.

Entire communities often moved en masse, a fact which implies that the network of emotional ties, the social glue that holds groups together, was considered indispensable to survival. If various groups depended on one another to help in the rituals considered necessary to ensure safety and maintain the world, if they truly believed that their prayers and rituals might affect rainfall and crops, they may have believed that in order to hold their ritual system together they had to stay together. This was likely true in many cases.

Cultures survived because of elaborate enfranchising stories, and rituals in which they acted out the reasons why they were who they were, where their ancestors had come from, and how to live gracefully. Stories and rituals held them whole as they suffered resettlement, always praying for rain, and struggled to keep believing in themselves.

CHAPTER FOUR

The Invasions: Spanish Swords, Christianity, and Americans

Then the growth of native cultures in the Southwest was profoundly interrupted. The Spanish arrived, armored warriors on horseback and Catholic priests, men interested in conquest, saving souls and rumors of fortunes for the taking. History arrived.

The first non-Indian in the Southwest was a black Spanish slave named Estéban. He survived the 1528 wreck of a sailing ship on the Florida coast, and with three Spaniards made his way around the Gulf of Mexico to Spain's colonial capital in Mexico City. The trip took eight years. Along the way Estéban became a shaman. In Mexico City he told stories of cities and gold. In 1529 he accompanied an expedition to find the seven golden (and nonexistent) cities of "Cíbola." What the Spaniards found was a Zuni village. The Zuni imprisoned Estéban and three days later killed him. But the seeds to another dream had been scattered, and they grew.

In 1540 the Spanish sent Francisco Vasquez de Coronado north with three hundred Spanish soldiers, eight hundred Indian servants, and herds of horses. On July 7, encountering people who became the present-day Zuni, Coronado demanded food. They refused; their village was sacked. Thirteen pueblos along the Rio Grande were destroyed and hundreds of Indians were burned at the stake over the next two years, before Coronado took his forces back to Mexico. A intermittent bitter war had commenced.

The Spanish crown, in 1598, having ordered that the natives be met with "peace, friendship, and good treatment" to enhance chances they might become Christians, sent Don Juan de Oñate north from Mexico to the Rio Grande valley with 129 soldiers, 7 friars, and 2 lay brothers. Oñate established seven missionary districts, ranging from Hopi to Taos and Pecos to El Paso, and named Nueva Mexico. But "peace, friendship and good treatment" soon went wrong, at Acoma. Oñate's nephew, a thug named Zaldivar, demanded food, climbed the 357-foot tower of rock to the pueblo with fourteen men, and began raiding supplies. The people at Acoma slaughtered them. Oñate struck back savagely, and six hundred people from Acoma were killed. Men over twenty-five had one foot cut off before being sent into bondage.

Seventy settlers arrived from Mexico in December 1600.

But they'd come to a land of deserts, no mineral wealth, and a native population who showed no interest in Christianity. Over the next decades Nueva Mexico languished, the military, friars, and settlers competing to exploit Indian labor and tribute. The settlers put the natives to work on their properties. The friars wanted both voluntary labor and for the pueblos to give up their native religions (the friars particularly abhorred what they took to be the devil worship practiced underground—in kivas). The political and military rulers seemed exclusively dedicated to amassing wealth they could take back to Mexico.

Severe drought in the late 1660s led to starvations and increasingly savage raids by the nomadic Apache and Comanche. By that time, 2,500 settlers and 30 friars lived in the midst of 15,000 native people in the pueblos along the Rio Grande and in Acoma, Zuni, and Hopi. Seemingly unable to realize the degree to which they were vulnerable, they governed with stunning arrogance.

In 1675 the military assisted friars in publicly whipping forty-three native religious leaders and hanging three others for encouraging idolatry. Native anger exploded during the summer of 1680, in the Pueblo Rebellion. Organized by a humiliated native priest named Pope, and a black slave named Naranjo, Indians in the pueblos across the northern Rio Grande valley struck early on the morning of August 10, 1680, with unprecedented unity.

The first death reported was that of a friar from the pueblo at Tesuque, just north of Santa Fe, Father Pio. He was killed by men he thought of as members of his flock. Over the next two days, along the Rio Grande and in pueblos to the west, Indians killed friars, burned missions, sacked haciendas, and drove settlers to safety behind walls in Santa Fe. The siege that ensued only ended when the military and settlers finally broke out and endured a long, degrading march to El Paso. The Pueblo Rebellion had accomplished its purposes. The hated Spaniards had been driven away.

But pueblo unity came apart, old hostilities were renewed, Apache raiding increased, pueblos were abandoned. The Spanish returned twelve years later.

This time the friars were no longer determined to eradicate kachinas and native religion. Indians were no longer punished for not going to Mass; they gathered in kivas and danced in their squares. The pueblo creator was after all not utterly different from the Christian god, nor were the pueblo goddesses so unlike the Virgin, nor were the kachinas entirely unlike angels. Mutual religious tolerance became a habit and is to this day.

Spanish settlement in southern Arizona came later, and accomplished less. The missionizing of a Jesuit named Eusebio Francisco Kino, from the 1680s to his death in 1711, resulted in little substantive change.

In 1767 Jesuits were banned from the New World, their place taken by the Franciscans. In 1775 an Irishman named Don Hugo O'Connor built a military post on the Santa Cruz River, the Presidio of San Augustín del Tucson. In 1783, south of Tucson, the Franciscans began building a twin-towered baroque, Moorish, and Byzantine church. Known as White Dove of the Desert, with vivid paintings on the walls and ceilings, and red, blue, yellow, silver, and gold painted statuary, it serves the Tohono O'odham Indians on the San Xavier Indian Reservation, and is a prime tourist destination these days.

That was as far into present-day Arizona as the Spanish settled. As a result, the Athapascan bands in the north, people who became the Navajo, were left on their own. Over time they adapted elements from the pueblos at Hopi and Zuni and along the Rio Grande, and from the Europeans. From the pueblos they took weaving and pottery-making. From the Spaniards they learned to herd cattle, sheep, and goats, to use metals and cotton. But the Spanish never converted the Navajo to Catholicism, or imposed much in the way of political control. The Navajo settled in and reinvented themselves as pastoralists. Their language remained intact, as did their religion, centered in their ceremonial six- or eight-sided hogans (which were built with short logs and thus suited to juniper-tree country).

By the middle of the eighteenth century, the raiders known as Apache had begun to settle. But not much changed among the Hispanic settlers. Many spoke sixteenth-century Castilian Spanish. Because iron for wagon-wheel rims was hard to come by, hauling was done with wooden-wheeled carts. In the fertile valley of the Rio Grande, from Santa Fe to Las Cruces, they farmed soils renewed each year by flooding, and developed a system in which communities elect a *mayordomo* or ditch boss, to oversee the distribution of irrigation water. Designed to ensure fairness in the use of a commons, it's an envied model around the world, and still in widespread use.

But as happens so often in isolated backlands, a defensive and repressive ruling-class culture was coalescing. At the top was an aristocracy claiming descent from Spain (some were Jews driven from Spain in the anti-Semitic wave around the time of Columbus).

The highest social rank was reserved for those born in Spain. Then came, in this ranking, "pure-blood" Spanish born in Mexico; *mestizos* of mixed Spanish and Mexican Indian blood; *coyotes,* the children of Spanish and New Mexican Indians; and *mulattos,* who were black and Spanish. Last were *genizaros,* enslaved children of the nomadic tribes who had been brought up Spanish and freed as adults.

Changes accumulated slowly. French and American mountain men and traders were coming in over the Santa Fe Trail. While their behavior was often outlandish, drunken, and barbaric, they brought new ideas, books, textiles, and medicines. Then in 1821 the people of New Spain overthrew the Spanish, creating the Republic of Mexico. All the people, Indians and Spanish of all varieties, were now citizens.

In 1845 the United States annexed the former Mexican state of Texas. On May 13, 1846, the United States declared war on Mexico itself. The 2,700-man Army of the West entered Santa Fe without opposition in mid-August and took possession of New Mexico. The Treaty of Guadalupe Hidalgo ended the Mexican-American War in 1848 and guaranteed land grants awarded by Spain to pueblo peoples, known as "barbarians." (The nomadic raiding tribes, the Comanche and the Apache and even the Navajo, who were by this time largely settled, were called "savages.")

The Navajo operated in bands, some settled and others wandered and raided. Treaties made with one band did not hold for the next. Because of this they were soon crossways with the United States military. In 1860 some two thousand Navajo in eastern Arizona attacked Fort Defiance. They suffered serious defeat, even though it looked for a while as if they had inexplicably won when the U.S. military abandoned forts throughout the region. But the other shoe was getting ready to drop.

In 1862 a column of U.S. troops arrived in Santa Fe from California. They were under orders to put an end to raiding by the "savages." Kit Carson, mountain man and scout, was hired out of retirement in Taos. It was Carson's task to round up the raiders into a forty-square-mile camp, Bosque Redondo ("round woods") on the Pecos River, where they would be converted into Christian farmers. After corralling the Mescalero Apache (some four hundred warriors and families), in 1866-67 Carson went after the Navajo. He soon destroyed their herds and reduced them to starvation in Canyon de Chelly. About eight thousand Navajo made the famous Long Walk, more than three hundred miles to Bosque Redondo; stragglers were shot or taken into slavery by New Mexicans.

The chance that Carson accepted but despised his role in these sad events is sensibly written about by Tom Dunlay in *Kit Carson and the Indians*. Col. John Chivington, after his Sand Creek massacre of two hundred Cheyenne, mostly women and children, claimed to be the greatest Indian fighter of all time. Carson said, "I don't like a hostile Red Skin better than any of you do. I've fit 'em—fout 'em—as hard as any man. But I never yit drew a bead on a squaw or papoose and I loath and hate the man who would...no one but a coward or a dog would do it."

After four years of confinement, after many had died, the six thousand Navajo who remained were marched back to a reservation in northwestern New Mexico. During this suffering, ironically, various bands began to understand that they together constituted the Navajo Nation, which would have the political power to protect the welfare of their people. Their reservation today is the size of West Virginia; 250,000 Navajo live there, the most populous tribe in the United States. Many are pastoral and most pursue an elaborate spiritual and ceremonial life. While many Navajo live in poverty, their beliefs and identity endure.

Change accelerated. The Butterfield Overland Mail Company opened a stage line from Missouri to San Francisco by way of El Paso, Tucson, and Los Angeles—a tough 26-day trip that cost two hundred dollars and passed through the territory of the Chiricahua Apache, who were led by a warrior named Cochise. Despite the deaths of drivers and passengers (the source of endless movie mythology), the line only once in its history missed coming in on schedule.

In the early 1860s a legendary prospector, Joseph Walker, found gold in the Bradshaw Mountains of Arizona, and mining towns sprang into being. Prescott and Jerome lasted; Bumble Bee and Vulture vanished. The remaining wild tribes were corralled onto reservations in the 1870s. They had to be fed, as did the miners. Cattlemen fought wars over the free range, the right to raise beef where they pleased. Gunfighters like Billy the Kid made their appearance in American mythology (another part of that history, of course, is a legacy of overgrazing, grasslands gone to cactus, cheatgrass, and brush).

In 1877 a loner named Edward Schieffelin discovered silver in southeastern Arizona. Tombstone was born. By 1881 it was the largest town in the Arizona Territory, four thousand citizens and two churches, a school, dance halls, brothels, saloons, gambling dens, mills and mines, thieves and more thieves. After a decade (more fodder for movies—Wyatt Earp and the Gunfight at the OK Corral), the mines began closing. Tombstone presently seems to subsist on the tourist business. It's said the longest shot that hit anybody at the OK Corral was twelve feet, with a shotgun. But you won't hear that story in Tombstone, where commercial interests live off six-gun legends.

In this overview of invasions it feels, as the nineteenth century ends, like one movement is over and the modern has not quite begun. So one more legendary story of a lost cause, that of the Chiricahua Apache, defeated and placed on the San Carlos Reservation, north of their ancestral lands, and their last outbreak, and the warrior named Geronimo.

The Chiricahua were capable of prodigious feats. They traveled fifty miles a day, found water, and then disappeared, only to strike again, days later, far away. Geronimo's last outbreak, in late 1885, was not so much dedicated to escaping the American military as to inflicting vengeance. By mid-1886, five thousand American soldiers were pursuing Geronimo and his band of thirty-four, a count which includes women and children. In September he surrendered, having been promised that after a few years in a Florida prison he would be returned to his people. But all the Chiricahua were sent to prison camps in Florida, and it was 1913 before any of them were allowed back into the Southwest. Geronimo, having spent decades as a tourist attraction at international expositions, died in 1909. There is today no culture known as Chiricahua Apache.

CHAPTER FIVE

Timeless in Our Time

One winter night in Las Vegas, in the Mirage Hotel parking lot, Annick and I witnessed the fabulous spitting of a faux-volcano. Inside, white tigers prowled a glassed-off cage. We sipped martinis with living orchids draped just over our heads. I honored my birth date (August 14) by playing a few dollars into the Leo machine in the row of horoscope slots (these people think of everything), and, abruptly, I won enough to buy a pair of first-rate sushi dinners with perhaps too much hot top-notch sake.

So it was with some dullness that Annick and I headed south into dark storms the next morning, crossing the Colorado at Hoover Dam, setting sail onto the flatlands of northern Arizona, intent on visiting native sites written up in our guidebooks. I was hungover but excited, a fragile state; over fifty years of age, I hadn't traveled much of anywhere; seeing the sights was still a new thing.

What I wasn't prepared to hunt out was much contact with living people. People in our southeastern Oregon outback didn't intrude into the lives of others, particularly strangers, an absolute respect for privacy which seems misguided to me now. It cuts off contact and contributes to the cloistered, xenophobic frigidity encountered in so many rural communities.

Native people, I told Annick, had talked to plenty of outsiders. I intended to leave them alone. She said I was nuts. "People love it if you're interested in their lives."

We had it in mind, first-off, to visit the Havasupai Indians, a tiny culture of maybe two hundred whose name means "People of the Blue-Green Water" in a paradise of deep canyons which descend to the Grand Canyon. But by midmorning it was raining steadily. We had no idea about the realities of what we were proposing. I must have read, in Wallace Stegner's *The Sound of Mountain Water*, of his trip to Havasu with Mary, and remembered "gardens bright with sinuous rills where blossoms many an incense-bearing tree." But I also must have repressed the part about riding down fourteen miles of rough trail as they descended thousands of feet, and that they'd brought their own food, and that the trip in and out each took a day. I'd forgotten that Stegner said "even Shangri-La has its imperfections." He told of tuberculosis, dysentery, and warned of "fatalistic apathy," and the way it can invade a society based on "repetition of simple routine" when that routine is "confounded and destroyed by contact with the civilization of white America." He hoped they survived.

In *Legends of the American Desert,* Alex Shoumatoff tells of a trip to Havasu when the Havasupai were growing marijuana and into Rastafarianism and reggae music to a degree that led Navajo to nickname the canyon Little Jamaica. Shoumatoff describes it as a "spoiled Eden" and "part paradise, part ghetto."

But most of all I'd neglected to notice that those trips had been taken in the summertime. Our rain was turning to spitting snow. So, reluctantly, we decided to put the miss on the Havasupai. Which was our good luck. We'd never have gotten in, and might have had trouble just getting back to the highway. Disappointing but I could live with it, that's what I thought, there were more down the road. Years later Annick finally got to Havasu Canyon in company with a group of women writers who were traveling the Grand Canyon by dory boat. She tells of a bright morning and waterfalls encased in travertine, and doesn't like hearing about an increasingly degraded, commodified paradise, tourists coming in for the day by helicopter.

Traveling the native Southwest we expect to encounter the nineteenth-century look we've seen in black-and-white photos, but there are contrails in the skies and plastic bags dangling from the cactuses. Which doesn't mean the native cultures have dissolved. They are, as we are, evolving.

Snow was falling heavily in late afternoon when Annick and I got to the tourist community at the South Rim of the Grand Canyon. We were luckier than we knew; some traveler canceled at the elegant old El Tovar Hotel. Instead of huddling in the car, stuck in a snowbank and freezing on the high rim of the canyon above Havasupai, where nobody lives, we were sampling desserts before a big fireplace, and then bundled in for the night.

Morning broke to perfect blue skies and eighteen inches of snow, which reached into the canyon in streaks for thousands of feet, into the reddish maze of towers and precipices above the river. We shuffled along on the edge of more distance to fall than I liked. Annick hung over the guardrail, a woman who loves heights. She says she knew at thirteen the West was home, a girl from Chicago at the head of a chairlift in Colorado on a clear morning, bright snowfields falling away on all sides, blessing her family for having brought her, breathing out wisps of mist.

But I was still dedicated to rushing. That afternoon we gazed across Tesigi Canyon and into the enormous overhanging, sheltering alcove of red stone under which ancient people built the cliff house called Betatakin. But we didn't take the five-hour hike to see the ruin close up—or consider an overnight camp out at Keet Seel, miles away. Not in midwinter (not ever in our lives so far as it turns out). We'd planned to see this cliff house as it faced into the warming winter sun and we were there, having done it.

What we didn't see were the aspen and oak in the canyon below where Douglas-fir and horsetail fern grow and where those people grew food. What we didn't take away was any sense of the difficulties overcome by the people who'd lived there so long ago. We'd tipped our hats but felt no real intimacy with what it had been like to be human there.

Content to think that I would get around to reflecting on these sights in tranquillity (which I only now, all these years later, as I write this book, seem to be getting around to), I was happy. And seriously wrongheaded. Intimacy with otherness is close to impossible without taking some time to stop playing the game of anthropologist.

By late afternoon we'd checked out the Navajo jewelry in hock to the trading-post grocery stores in the wind-blown town of Kayenta and were whirling along on the 17-mile loop road through Monument Valley. We saw red-rock spires and buttes rising four or five or six hundred or so feet above the valley and silhouetted against a sunset coloring thin clouds that turned from faint yellow to deep orange striped with red. We smiled at formations called the Mittens (fingers pointing to the sky), and walked out from the North Window and stood in the luminous twilight, moved by the sight of mesas towering into evening without fathoming why.

Surprised by ordinary life, we saw a boy galloping along on a bareback bay horse. He paid us no attention, and went off into a dark arroyo. Another way to live was going on nearby, but I had no idea what it might be like, or how to find out.

After driving an hour or so into the falling night, across empty flatlands, to Chinle and the mouth of Canyon de Chelly, we made our stand in Thunderbird Lodge, and had a beer and some authentic Navajo cafeteria cooking. But we didn't know that we should have put up at Gouldings Lodge, out behind a six-hundred-foot red-rock tower in Monument Valley. We could have spent the next morning on a guided tour, we could have known enough to make reservations, we could have tried making conversation with the deeply traditional people who'd lived in Monument Valley all their lives, we could have gone there knowing something of what they believe about the place where they've lived. Instead, I at least was semi-emptyheaded.

Sitting in the cafeteria at Thunderbird Lodge, Annick eyed me with distance in her eyes. "Get ready for some hiking," she said, "tomorrow is going to be different."

Find the good books, that's my idea, not just the guidebooks. Read them, mark them up, use them as tools, carry them with you. No place can be real emotionally unless we've imagined the life there, and our imagining is not likely to be very substantive if not informed.

So, some history. In 1880, Benjamin Wetherill and his Quaker family moved to ranchlands along the Mancos River, nearby to an unexplored southern Colorado highland called Mesa Verde. Richard Wetherill, the eldest of five sons, became famous in archaeological circles.

Gathering cattle in the Mesa Verde canyons on a cold December afternoon in 1888, Richard and a brother-in-law came on a concentration of cliff dwellings—Square Tower House, Spruce Tree House, and the Cliff Palace—now centerpiece exhibits in Mesa Verde National Park. Richard and his brothers eventually found 182 sites on Mesa Verde. Richard led academic expeditions not only to Mesa Verde but off into the Grand Gulch area of Utah and to Chaco Canyon. He found Keet Seel but missed Betatakin (his brother John found it years later), and was the first to discover that a people we call Basketmakers had lived in the Southwest two thousand years before the Anasazi (the vivid enigmatic pictographs at Green Mask Springs and Jailhouse Ruin and Horseshoe Canyon were done by Basketmakers). One of the ways the Wetherill brothers made a living was by selling artifacts they found, and their findings anchor Southwestern collections at the Field Museum in Chicago, the American Museum of Natural History, and the National Museum of the American Indian.

While he's been criticized for being a commercial pot-hunter, Richard Wetherill knew his way around the country where he lived with unequaled intimacy, and in his way revered the archaeological treasures he found. Like anyone, he aspired to significance. Eventually he lived at Chaco Canyon and promoted himself as a responsible archaeologist, proposing to excavate and reconstruct Pueblo Bonito. But Richard was killed from ambush, either by angry natives or his wife's cowboy lover, before that dream could be realized. This story is told in detail in a good book: *Richard Wetherill: Anasazi* by Frank McNitt.

In Search of the Old Ones by David Roberts tells of retracing Richard Wetherill's explorations, and of Roberts's own discoveries, bowls, and baskets, which he left where he found them, deep in hidden crevices in hidden canyons. Outraged by heedless desecrations at Lake Powell, Roberts says the sporting life there is equivalent to "water-skiing in a cathedral." Beauty drowned in order that golf courses and lawns in urban metroplexes can be overwatered, economic development overshadowing all else. And Roberts is simply correct. His anger led me to daydreaming about hidden mysteries in Grand Gulch and Cedar Mesa, difficult canyonland territories I've driven by, where I might have gone if I'd been tough and ambitious enough. But which "hidden mysteries" would those be? Why would they seem significant? What do I (we) want from the deep past?

The answer, I think, is simple enough. We want to understand the story of how we became what we are, and another even more important story, about how all the people who exist and have existed are irrevocably alike in their fragilities, a story in which it becomes obvious that we need to cherish one another because we are alone otherwise, which might incite some of us to take care of one another and glories and ecologies. A story of people just like ourselves, who were also intent on survival. We see ourselves mirrored in them, and our own situation in the long isolations and happy enclosures they inhabited. We seek stories to use as weight to anchor our minds when we begin to drift.

In 1910 John and Louisa Wetherill (Hosteen John and Slim Woman as they were know to the Navajo) set up a tent in the snow at Kayenta when Kayenta was farther from a railroad than any other "white" settlement in the United States. They established a post to trade with the Indians, and made a life of it. John discovered Betatakin, and like Richard he guided archaeologists. In 1913, ex-President Theodore Roosevelt came to Kayenta on an expedition to Rainbow Bridge. He stayed with the Wetherills, and wrote them up in an article published in *Outlook* magazine. Cartoonist George Herriman read the article, and went to Kayenta. Eagerly, it might be said, since he'd traveled through northern Arizona on the railroad years earlier and found the look and speed of things there to his liking. Herriman took an interest in the Navajo, loafed through long working vacations, and eventually returned twenty-some times.

Herriman's classical comic strip, "Krazy Kat"—modernist and whimsical, affectionate and satiric, about a brick-throwing love affair between a cat and a mouse—is set in what Umberto Eco called "surrealist inventions, especially in the improbable lunar landscape." Eco meant the desert around Kayenta and in Monument Valley, lonesome metaphoric towers reaching to the empty sky, and the unlikely romance enacted nearby.

"Krazy Kat" is about life as play, in mysterious playing fields given us by the mysterious universe. And about love. In one of the brilliant essays in *Great Topics of the World,* Albert Goldbarth quotes the Kat as saying, "In my Kosmos, there will be no feeva of discord." George Herriman was a genius I'd like to have known. "Krazy Kat" is a true mudhead comic strip, given to undermining our gone-dead status quo; it's high and sprightly and spirited reinventive storytelling.

In 1921 a tall man named Harry Goulding moved to Monument Valley. Except for the Wetherills in Kayenta, twenty-five miles to the south, Goulding and his wife, Leona, nicknamed Mike, were the only whites in permanent residence for hundreds of miles. The next four years they lived in tents. They tended sheep, traded with the Navajo, and accumulated the money, by 1936, to buy their land. In 1938, hearing that a movie was going to be shot near Flagstaff, Harry went to Los Angeles, saw the director, and sold him on the idea of filming in Monument Valley.

The director was John Ford, and his movie, which established Ford's reputation as a first-string director, was *Stagecoach,* a quintessentially western American drama about strangers out to reestablish themselves in a lost land, red stone fingers pointing to the heavens like signposts above a paradise.

John Ford liked Monument Valley, despite the rough accommodations, and he liked the Gouldings. He returned time after time, film after film. There's a famous sequence in *My Darling Clementine,* the floor of a half-built church in a movie version of Tombstone put to use as a communal dance hall, in which I see the essence of what Ford was trying for, gunfighters and good country people celebrating the chance that they might possibly be able to invent a good and decent life for themselves—even with those stone fingers pointing heavenward as if to indicate that paradise is always elsewhere. Even if hero, Henry Fonda playing Wyatt Earp, rides off unflinching and alone into the usual hero's stoic emotional isolations.

I might have thought about those conjunctions in and around Monument Valley if I'd read books, as travelers should. I'd have known walking to Havasu in midwinter was a ridiculous notion, and that we'd need days if we hoped to grow into any feel for Monument Valley and the Navajo people who live there, if we wanted to converse there in some other than a turista capacity, if I had any hope of enlarging my blundering life. Three or four hours, stopping by on the run (as we did), a man with any wit should have known, wouldn't start to cut it.

The next morning was indeed, as Annick had promised, different. We parked on the south rim of Canyon de Chelly and hiked down over looming thousand-foot cliffs to the White House. With plastic sacks over our shoes, we waded sandbar to sandbar across a creek in ankle-deep water. (On a later trip

Annick was crippling along on a healing ankle and I had to carry her across the creek on my back, an occasion she regards as hilarious in memory.) We listened to winds breathing over the enormous face of water-stained rock above us. Annick said she heard bells, maybe Navajo sheep, or eternity resonating. She voted in favor of eternity.

The White House, a few decaying mud-brick rooms on a rocky shelf, must have been a stunning place to live. Parked at the overlook we encountered a young couple deep into all-the-way lovemaking in the seat of a Chevy pickup truck. I took their devotions as a message about the value of primordial glory.

But still I wonder at the difficulty involved in living at the White House. And I wondered why those people left. Did life under those cliffs remind them too insistently of mortality? Or what? Who were their enemies? Did they just get tired of hauling water?

Each brick, shaped down by the creek, had to be brought up ladders and toe- and handholds to the shelf. They must have been deeply fearful to consider living on that cliffside, where children were in constant danger of falling off.

At what costs has social order been maintained by Southwestern tribes? How have their cultures survived inside our relentlessly invasive national society? To what degree are they alike?

For openers they've inherited a system of complex ongoing rituals in which every person has a responsible role. Rituals embody religion, and are performed to ensure individual and societal well-being. Taking part in religious and practical efforts of your people to survive, giving away both time and effort, is understood as normal behavior.

Elaborate communal rituals sanctify vital relationships between communities and the natural world, communities and other communities, between clans, moieties, and families, and between individuals. All relationships.

Alfonso Ortiz, a University of New Mexico anthropologist who grew up at San Juan Pueblo, wrote in "Ritual Drama and the Pueblo World View" that the "undulating rhythms of nature govern their whole existence, from the timing and order of ritual dramas to the planning of economic activities." He goes on to say that "everything in the cosmos is knowable and being knowable, controllable" by "letter-perfect attention to detail and performance, thus the Pueblo emphasis on formulas, ritual, and the repetition revealed in ritual drama."

In "Landscape, History, and the Pueblo Imagination," Leslie Marmon Silko, a poet, novelist, and MacArthur Fellow from Laguna Pueblo, says "Survival depended on harmony and cooperation not only among human beings, but among all things." Silko says Pueblo peoples saw themselves "as part of an ancient continuous story composed of innumerable bundles of other stories.

"They instinctively sorted events and details into a loose narrative structure. Everything became a story." Traditionally everyone, from the youngest child to the oldest person, was expected to listen and to be able to recall or tell a portion, if only a small detail, from a narrative account or story. Thus the remembering and retelling were a communal process.

"The ancient Pueblo people sought a communal truth, not an absolute." Which is appealing these days, truth in absolute forms being increasingly suspect. We might settle for stories that bring us together in order that, as Silko says, "the terror of facing the world alone is extinguished."

Native cultures in the Southwest have historically been profoundly conservative, fearing change for social and religious reasons. Rituals enacted at Zuni or Taos or Hopi or among the Navajo and Apache would be recognizable to men and women who've been dead for generations. They have been tested over and over and slowly evolved. These days men and women talk on cell phones as they prepare for seasonal rituals; they clearly understand these rituals to be the sacred basis for the survival of their people, as did their ancestors.

One travel fantasy goes this way—buy an Airstream trailer, hook it up behind a heavy-duty four-wheel-drive pickup truck. Home would be trailing behind, the world before you each day.

But I've never seriously considered going deep into hock for an Airstream. Annick and I hum along in my Honda. Over years we've learned to eat in village cafés and talk to barmaids in roadside taverns, walk under cottonwood trees on riverbanks and lie us down to sleep in plywood motels. We find our way, we're together, and often manage to be very pleased with what we're doing.

But going alone! Crossing pale deserts and ascending red-rock canyons into the juniper-green foothills, distant piney mountains lying blue in the distances, is another matter. I've spent decades trying to get it right.

Punching nervously at the radio, I listen to distant Navajo voices, salsa music from the border towns, and ultra right-wing nitwit talk-show gurus. I play Beethoven's sublime "Archduke Trio" and bluegrass on the CD deck but don't really listen, then stop in taverns to make lonely guy-talk with bartenders. But that's a pathetic game, so I keep moving.

Stop, I tell myself, walk out into the countryside, leave your automobile and the highway entirely out of sight, and study the varieties of cactus, small birds as they nest, listen to the silences. But I don't. Existential spooks are too much with me. This isolation, they whisper, is what's real. Get used to it. But I flee.

On a Sunday morning, just lately, I had another encounter with reeducation. In Santa Fe, the writer Frederick Turner and his wife, Alise, told me to contact a Navajo woman they admired, Gloria Emerson, and I did. Gloria offered to take me to meet a Navajo medicine man named Mister Jim, to talk about mountain gods. Southwestern native cultures, after centuries of exposure to Christianity, go on resolutely believing in gods who inhabit mountaintops.

Gloria and I drove past the volcanic extrusion called Shiprock—rising seventeen hundred feet above the flats, it can be thought of as resembling a sailing ship—and into Arizona. South from the highway we followed a gravel road, which led us through scatters of juniper into foothills.

"He's very busy," Gloria said. "He can only talk to you for a half hour." Mister Jim, it seemed, spent his Sundays on curing ceremonies. I am not a mystical man, and my skepticism was blooming.

What we came to, amid the juniper, was a blue-gray Navajo hogan, doorway as always facing east, to the sunrise. A four-wheel-drive minivan was parked before the hogan. Gloria told me to park alongside, precisely parallel to the minivan. She sat with her eyes downcast, her hands folded in her lap. "We'll wait," she said.

Eventually two long-haired, unshaven men came out. "Don't look," Gloria said. "Don't meet their eyes." I wondered if they were dangerous until they got in the minivan and drove away. Then a young couple in a dusty Plymouth pulled in beside us. They didn't look at us. These transactions did not seem so much dangerous as polite. A man came out of the hogan. He gestured to Gloria.

"Now," she said, "we can go in." The couple in the dusty Plymouth was destined to wait. We didn't look at them.

The interior of the dirt-floored hogan was almost empty—without decoration, rugs folded along the walls, a plastic chair for anyone not comfortable sitting on the rugs. (I sat on the chair, Gloria on a rug.)

Mister Jim was calm and deliberate, in his middle years, and he sat in his traditional place, on the folded rugs, his back against the wall directly across from the door that opened to the east. "What do you want?" he asked.

I said I wasn't sure, and Gloria explained that I was interested in the Navajo relationship to their land, that I had asked her how people managed to embrace the isolations involve in herding sheep month after month, winter after winter, spending their nights in a hogan lost in the midst of the mostly uninhabited deserts and hills.

What he knows, Gloria said, speaking of me, is what he's seen from the highway, and in photographs, and what he's read. He sees lost harmonies and denuded lives. (Gloria said something to that effect; no notetaking or tape recording was permitted.)

Mister Jim ignored us in a moment of silence, then spoke for twenty minutes. Navajo belief, he told me, centers around four sacred mountains, north, south, east, and west. An elaborate set of mythological teaching stories proceeds from those mountains. Stories connected to the western mountain, for instance, instruct the Navajo in ways to live a proper social life. They are about marriage and children, and how to live in family and in community and in the entire Navajo Nation, with dignity and love and forbearance. Sacred stories connected to gods on their specific mountains, he said, tell us these things. The land tells us these things. Stories, he said, help us know who we are, and how to conduct and sustain ourselves.

His clan, Mister Jim told me, included the stars in their patterns, the mountains and their gods, the quiet around in the deserts, and this his sacred homeplace, the shrine out in the juniper where he held ceremonies, this hogan and the house where he lived with his family, his fields where corn grew, his horses and his cattle and sheep out on the deserts, grazing. It's all sacred and it's alive. This hogan, he said, is alive. People have lived here since time immemorial, and things go on changing because they're alive. But they also go on as they always have, through death, rebirth, spring, and winter.

Mister Jim was forthright and patient in his explanations. There could be no possible profit for him in taking this time with me, but I couldn't understand what he was saying as other than mysticism until Gloria and I left and had driven higher up into the Carrizo Mountains. We parked amid ragged stands of juniper and stood gazing down as patterns of clouds and sunlight drifted over the deserts toward Monument Valley, which was just beyond the western horizon.

Gloria must have sensed that I was baffled. "Think of the mountains as books," she said. "They tell us things, just as books instruct people." Listening to ringing silence as patterns of light flowed out before me, I thought maybe this listening was the beginning of what Mister Jim meant by talking to gods.

Maybe the gods would tell me that mirroring systems, what physicists call fractals, from stars to our lives, are what is, and that they are, as alive as anything; and that I can thus never be all the way alone and that this is as far as solace goes. But actually, I was hearing my own thoughts.

A couple of days later, in Santa Fe, Fred Turner gave me an essay he'd written about a French vintner, Alain Querre, who practiced his art in the Bordeaux region. Querre said that a vintner "must above all know and live his soil." Fred wrote that "the tending of vines had something of the sacred about it" and went on to say, "It was a matter of understanding, in the moment of holding your glass, the whole complex process: the microclimate of the soil that grew the grapes, the varietals planted there, the sort of care these required, the attitudes of the men and women who harvested them, the whole ancient tradition of producing fine wines." He concludes by saying that drinking a glass of that wine is "a sort of sacrament."

What did I take from Gloria and Mister Jim? Maybe this: There are Bordeaux wine gods and gods at Chaco Canyon and star gods in those lavender velvet night skies over the American Southwest, red-rock gods and hummingbird gods flitting among the gray-white sycamore along Cave Creek in the Chiricahua Mountains, gods of the Mexican wolf and the puma, gods of cooking and sheep herding and fixing fence and irrigating corn, gods of tradition and decorum and taking care all around. Mountain gods, gods of mescal and hot peppers and intimacy, gods and gods and gods, all whispering the simple message, "The world is alive to us if we can love it." Which is what I find myself thinking.

Having bought some ears of variously colored corn, for kitchen decorations in Montana, and a brilliantly patterned red sash, Annick and I walked among ancient houses at Old Orabi, the oldest Hopi village. I wondered why a simple life like this (an inherently stupid thought, there are no simple lives) couldn't be enough. The reason was obvious—because I believe in the need to constantly reinvent ourselves, in the usefulness of staying up on our toes, the need for incessant rethinking of our purposes and strategies. But there can be too much staying up on our toes. It can lead to fretful, aimless, and frenetic social hopping and bopping, driven by a fear of what might happen if we ever slowed down. What if we went to sleep at the switch, or at the wheel, and fell behind, or crashed? Or simply noticed that we weren't up to much beyond staying on our toes?

The Hopi, on the other hand, believe in repetitions and order. I recalled a story from *Native American Testimony* edited by Peter Nabokov, told by Peter Nuvamsa, Sr. Confronting hippies who had taken to hanging around the Hopi mesas, Nuvamsa asked, "Why are you here? Why do you behave this way, doing anything that comes into your head? We do not like the way you are behaving. It's not our way. It's improper."

They said, "What's wrong with what we're doing? We are here because we're on your side. You have been put down by the establishment, and we are against the establishment." I told them, "No, you are not on our side. You don't behave well. Whatever you want, you take it. Whatever you want to do, you do it. There are rules in the world. You can't be just anything you want."

The Hopi, in short, as I get it, do not think of themselves as a counterculture. They believe in responsibility. They believe droughts and epidemics are the predictable result of conduct on the part of Hopi leaders and Hopi society. They live in a coherent, practical one-to-one trade-off relationship with sacredness, and still they are certainly among the most religious people in the world.

The Hopi focus on encouraging rain for the corn. Without rain there is no corn, and soon, no Hopi. That, most basically, is how they understand transactions with their Rain Gods. In *Legends of the American Desert,* Alex Shoumatoff says, "The scant rainfall on which their survival depends will only come through prayer, through everybody's heart being right.

"The Hopi believe...that when they die they become benevolent beings known as kachinas and eventually take the form of clouds, becoming Cloud People, whose substance, or *navala,* is liquid and is manifested as rain. As Cloud People who

send down their life-giving fluid to their kin, the dead continue to play a vital role in the order of things. Their kin must
perform certain ceremonies and smoke pipes known as cloud-
blowers before they plant their corn. They must summon the
Cloud People and beseech them to release their navala."
Shoumatoff says he learned these things from books. Hopi people, even when asked directly, are seriously disinclined to tell
white outsiders much about sacred matters.

Down the road a few miles at the Hopi Cultural Center, I
bought a mudhead clown kachina with erect penis blooming
from his forehead. It sounds obscene and ugly, but I took it to
be in the spirit of mudheads, unflinchingly ironic. "Life," I said
to the Hopi carver, thinking to connect. "Yeah," he said, smiling as he took my Visa card.

Old photographs of Southwestern native villages can be beguil-
ing because they seem to reveal a precisely realized dream. Alex
Shoumatoff on the other hand says the Hopi villages remind
him of Tibet—the wrinkled faces of very old women, snowy
peaks on the faint horizons, nothing much to see, not much
going on but a life which is none of our business.

The Hopi are among the few precontact cultures surviving
in the United States. Their society evolved through more than
four hundred years of precontact isolation and the four hundred
and fifty years since. Their struggle to survive lead them to
develop intricate ceremonies and rituals in which everything is
secondary to that main duty—beseeching, praying to, entreat-
ing, haranguing the rain gods.

After first contact with the Spanish in 1541 they survived unspeakable brutalities, hands and feet cut off and deaths as a result of whippings by white authorities. But most extraordinarily they survived the smallpox epidemics which took their population from around 7,500 in 1775 to 798 five years later.

Hopi culture is, obviously, enormously resilient, a toughness which to a great degree derives from their stabilizing religious life. The Hopi villages, while keeping to a culture-wide model, organize their own ceremonies. Their ceremonies—more than one a month—cycle through two periods.

The masked cycle, featuring elaborately costumed kachinas, runs from late winter to July, when the last of the corn has been planted. An unmasked cycle then lasts until the most important ceremony of all, Soyal, the winter solstice when the sun turns back toward the Hopi and the pueblo is cleansed of past misfortune and seed corn is sanctified in the kivas, and a new cycle of prayer begins.

Here, a bibliographic note: The religions of the Southwestern tribes are oftentimes profoundly interesting, and their ceremonies are usually emotionally resonant to any even mildly responsive witness, but there are dozens and dozens of kachinas, and literally thousands of ceremonial gestures, too many for me to explain if I could (and I can't). Anyone hoping to thoroughly understand the native cultures of the Southwest, not to speak of developing an empathetic relationship to any of them, might begin with the Smithsonian Institution's *Handbook of North American Indians, Volume 9: Southwest,* which also treats, among others, the Zuni and Rio Grande pueblos. The Navajo and Apache are considered in volume 10, also called *Southwest.*

In an essay called "Hopi World View," Louis A. Hieb tells us that the Hopi understand that "life and death, day and night, summer and winter are seen not simply as opposed but as involved in a system of alternation and continuity—indeed in a fundamental consubstantiality. Death is 'birth' into a new world."

This world and that of the gods are mirrors of each other and transactions between them involve reciprocal exchange— the Hopi feed the kachinas, and the kachinas feed the Hopi by bringing the rain. "Everything, in Hopi belief, is dependent on rainfall, which, when confined with Mother Earth, is the essence of all things."

We read our books and examine old photos and walk the contemporary Hopi mesas and talk to the people, and feel for a hopeful moment that in the mirror of what it's like to be human provided by the Hopi, we can see a chance for peace in our worldwide community. But connection is tricky, and not just because of Hopi reticence. On Second Mesa, in the village of Walpi, a man came up while I was walking the balustrade around the edge of the mesa, and offered to explain the Hopi beliefs. I imagined he was hitting on me, running some scam, and I turned away.

There are no more than seventy-five feet from the cliffs on one side of Walpi to the cliffs on the other. The accumulation of stonework and adobe buildings is stacked in that narrow space in a rough way that suggests to my metaphor-making consciousness they're of the cliffs themselves, i.e., authentic. I counted five kivas and nine clan houses among the Walpi. These people, in villages, clans, lineages, and kivas, house groups and clan groups, I thought, isolated in my self-administered defeat, are never alone. What do they know?

Walpi, inherently elemental, so obviously made of earth, like Acoma and the White House, is a situation in which I feel, immediately upon leaving, that I missed whatever it was that I went there to encounter.

So go back, I think, talk to people, this time get it right. But I don't get it right, any more than I can pin down my feelings as I stood viewing my mother's powered face that last time before she was interned. I'm drawn to Walpi by old photos and the fact that Walpi looks much the same as it did a hundred years ago, by a sense of deathlessness, the primordial dream.

"Corn cobs and husks, the rinds and stalks and animal bones," Leslie Marmon Silko writes, "were not regarded by the ancient people as filth or garbage. The remains were merely resting at midpoint in their journey back to dust. Human remains are not so different."

Silko says, "Rocks and clay are part of the Mother. They emerge in various forms, but at some time before, they were very small particles or great boulders. At a later time they may become what they once were. Dust." I imagine some mudhead Hopi clown-figure telling me, laughing, "Lighten up, old Sport, you are not going anywhere, your electricities will be around so long as there are electricities. Breathe and smile as the clouds drift over the desert."

And stop ignoring the obvious. What Walpi whispers into our suspicious minds, of course, if there must be a message, is simple: Be communal, join up, share your goods, and once in a while give your sweet time away, no charge, pro bono, and you'll be as close to home as you're likely to be. But is that exactly what we want to hear?

Hopi and the Zuni pueblos share one obvious thing: isolation. Traveling to Zuni, going alone, I zoomed on and on across plains. But Zuni was unlike Walpi. Zuni was not the elegant, stacked, and laddered pueblo I'd seen in hundred-year-old photographs. Rather, it was a cluster of cinder block houses, grocery stores, and shops selling native pots, carved silver jewelry, and fetishes. Cell phones looked to be a big consumer item, and TV dishes.

Hoping to buy a something for Annick, I wandered into a jewelry shop with a half-dozen motorcycles, road bikes, in front. The riders, in dusty leathers, chatted in French, joking with the Zuni proprietor while a lean woman with streaked blond hair, and burly tattooed fellow, tried on earrings. I drove on to Gallup, where I drank some gin, ate a chicken-fried steak smothered in sausage gravy, and sat in a motel room watching "America's War Against Terrorism" on the TV while a digital clock clicked off minutes.

The belief system that sustains Zuni, that I entirely missed, can be sensed in Dennis Tedlock's essay "Zuni Religion and World View" in the *Handbook of North American Indians*. The Zuni, Tedlock tells us, believe that the world is inhabited by "raw people" and "cooked people" (also known as "daylight people" and dependent on cooked food). The raw people eat food that is raw or has been sacrificed to them by the cooked people, and they can also change forms; they are people in the sense that one of their possible forms is human, and because they and humans should behave as kinsmen toward one another.

"The earth itself," Tedlock says, "is a raw person, Earth Mother; trees and bushes are her arms and hands, and she wears a robe of yellow flowers (pollen grains) in the summer and white flowers (snowflakes) in the winter." In return for prayers and offerings the Sun Father grants blessings to daylight people, including daylight itself. The daylight people have a similar reciprocal relationship to raw people like rainstorms, bears, kachinas, and corn plants.

Eliza McFeely, in *Zuni and the American Imagination*, sums up reasons why outsiders, reacting to incoherence in their own cultures, have found Zuni attractive. "Interdependent secret societies, each of which was concerned with a different aspect of Zuni's physical, economic, and spiritual health, were the cornerstones of Zuni social cohesion.

"The pueblo itself, in its courtyards, passageways, and rooftops, was stage and gallery for the kachina dances that were the most public of Zuni's religious practices." All the people, as participant or witness, were involved. "At times the entire village was transformed into a sort of open-air cathedral."

Social cohesion, I think, is the operative notion. Zuni religious life, as does most native religious life over the Southwest, because life in that arid land has been so precarious, centers on systems of caretaking of people, animals, plants, all of creation—and is thus inherently conservative.

In *Patterns of Culture*, published in 1934, anthropologist Ruth Benedict describes the Zuni culture as "Apollonian," restrained, more concerned with social order than individual desires, but essentially benevolent. In a radically disrupted world, such as that of recent times, as Eliza McFeely writes, the Zuni "emphasis on tradition, harmony, and the life of the social group" looked to be "a rational alternative."

But life is ordinarily disordered. In *The Beautiful and the Dangerous,* Barbara Tedlock tells of the seasons she and her husband spent working as anthropologists at Zuni. Her book is organized like a novel, scenes in progression, focused on the textures of daily life, meaning revealed in events. Toward the end she juxtaposes a boozy dance-hall night in Gallup with the masked Zuni dance ceremony called Shalako, each a search, each disturbed by conflicted yearnings. The Zuni, it seems, despite their famed rationality and concern for social order, also like to kick back and party.

But their losses are never entirely forgotten. Native American poet Joy Harjo, in "Deer Dancer," tells of barroom women in a scene like Gallup, fighting despair and finding meaning even after "the real world collapses." The last stanzas go like this:

> And then she took off her clothes. She shook loose memory, waltzed with the empty lover we'd all become.

> She was the myth slipped down through dreamtime. The promise of feast we all knew was coming. The deer who crossed through knots of a curse to find us. She was no slouch, and neither were we, watching.

The music ended. And so goes the story. I wasn't there.
But I imagined her like this, not a stained red dress
with tape on her heels but the deer who entered our
dream in white dawn, breathed mist into pine trees, her
fawn a blessing of meat, the ancestors who never left.

"How shall we enjoy ourselves," writes Dennis Tedlock, is a primary Zuni concern. "Many kachina dances are not so much sacred as they are beautiful." Barbara Tedlock tells of a bright and talented young Zuni potter, a single mother who is depressed and allows her infant daughter to almost suffocate while strapped to a cradleboard. The young woman says she wishes she could move to Albuquerque and "get an office job or something." She'd like to throw away all her security inside Zuni for an escape into the chancy Anglo world where she could maybe learn to be a real artist. Is that it?

Her mother then tells her, "If that's what you want to do, to run away, why, that's yours. But as for Lorinda, you'll be leaving her with us."

Our homes are a primary source of identity; without them to inhabit in our imaginations we often become disoriented. We wonder where are we, who are we, who should we be? But homes can also be an entrapment.

Southwestern native peoples have maintained the integrity of their communities without sacrificing individual spontaneity by insisting on belief that the world is alive if difficult, and that we have no choice but to meet life with life— working, cherishing, playing, dancing, and praying, thus keeping the world alive. At the same time, of course, some

of the most imaginative are looking for a way to get themselves to Albuquerque.

Southwestern villages like Hopi and Zuni have seemed like an
attractive alternative to our fractured culture for more than a
century. As a consequence the life-styles and arts of these communities are being copied, essentially commodified, by communal hippies and in high-end galleries in Santa Fe and Scottsdale.

Wandering the ancient mesa-top village of Acoma, I
bought Annick a necklace. But not many people live up there
full-time anymore. They are more comfortable in semi-Anglo
villages on the flatlands nearby. As are most citizens of Laguna,
down the highway toward Albuquerque. Many of the pueblos
have evolved into cultural museums, backdrops used by people
with art for sale to lure tourists. But nevertheless, the necklace
I bought for Annick was pure silver and beautifully crafted.

At the Hubbell Trading Post in Ganado, south of Canyon
de Chelly, there are stacks of brilliantly designed and finely
made Navajo rugs. The prices are high and should be.
Designing and weaving those rugs is an art learned over life-
times by women in hogans out amid the distances. Each rug,
after the design is thought out, takes hundreds of hours of slow,
intricate work.

But rug weaving is not an ancient Navajo art form. Rather,
with the encouragement of traders like Lorenzo Hubbell at
Ganado more than a hundred years ago, Navajo women developed rug weaving as a commercial enterprise. The weavers,
however, have let their vision and work evolve into a source of

both personal and community pride and identity, transforming what could have been the drudgery of "forced" work for hire into the high and voluntary artistic achievement their rugs so often are.

Be careful, take your time, and if you want to buy Navajo rugs or pueblo pottery or Hopi kachina dolls or Zuni jewelry and fetishes, learn to know what you like and why. There's junk everywhere—in Gallup it's possible to find lots of pseudo-Zuni art made in Mexico and the Philippines. But exquisite things can be found if you're prepared to pay uptown prices for an embodied vision.

CHAPTER SIX

The Santa Fe Triangle

My first time in Santa Fe was at a convention of the people who wrote pop-Western gunfighter novels. I was staying in very posh digs, elegant rooms, a laid-back open-to-the-night bar, and hyperexpensive Western art and native craft shops along an arcade. But the convention was brain-dead. I listened to talks about morality by old fellows who wrote shoot-'em-up pornography, bare-assed splendor in the meadow about every twenty pages, and to ecstatic theorizing about aesthetics by women wearing way too much silver, clanking squash-blossom necklaces and dozens of bracelets. This all seemed fraudulent, dedicated to selling a sort of imitation West.

And I felt like as big a fraud. The Western had always been a more or less ridiculous transmogrification of actual life in the West, and it wasn't even a vital commercial form anymore. And we all knew it. So I drank, and was happy when a wild fellow I'd known in other circumstances showed up with a crazed renegade painter who lived alone in the deep New Mexico outback, a man who was trying to get his beloved—ten thousand varieties of light playing over one particular run of infinities—onto canvas.

But before long a sourness descended over our group. We were absolutely unknown artists, and likely to stay that way. We seethed with envy, and took to stalking along the arcade, carrying drinks and making sarcastic remarks about the paintings and pottery on display there.

Then the crazed painter stuck his fist through the face of an enormous stereotypical acrylic cowboy on a buckskin horse who was eyeing the glory of a vast white to orange to deep red sunset, a work of art valued at three thousand dollars. Security appeared, in the form of a big uniformed balding man wearing a badge and a holstered weapon.

So, there in fact, before us, we had one of the essential conflicts in the West—inauthenticity, or not? But it turned out that the crazed painter, or the other fellow, I never did get it straight, was married to a woman with money. Credit cards appeared, and what had looked like serious trouble went away in moments.

The manager of the gallery smirked and winked at me as our group headed back toward the bar. "Those fellows," he said, "aren't they the real thing." It didn't seem to be a question. "What a hell of a town," he said. We were all of us, even him, in his mind, larger than life. In hindsight it seems clear we were up to nothing but self-justifying inauthenticities. However, the mudhead says, aren't we always, mostly?

A couple of years later Annick and I started our day in Santa Fe with room after room of Georgia O'Keeffe paintings in the museum off the square dedicated to her work—vividly feminine flowers and striped rose-and-saffron escarpments stretched out like a resting body and alive, and bone-white skulls juxtaposed against the blue purity in the sky. That vision is striking and entirely hers but in its commodified form, on framed posters all over Santa Fe, it's clichéd decor.

So, looking for sights we hadn't seen before, we went out for what we've come to think of as "the famous four-culture drive." North of Santa Fe we visited the Santuario de Chimayó, said to be the Lourdes of America. It's visited by thousands of mostly Hispanic and Indian pilgrims on Holy Week, some hiking or hitchhiking over hundreds of miles bearing hand-hewn crosses. Annick bought a tiny stamped tin milagro, which means "miracle" in Spanish, a head which when blessed might reinforce my resolve to stop smoking.

In the village of Chimayó I bought an elegant blanket from Trujillo's Weaving Shop, where they were being made as we watched. A friend told me that Chimayó has since become "the black-tar heroin capital of New Mexico," and that Espanola, down on the Rio Grande, has the highest percentage of overdose deaths of any population in the United States. What to say? Was this the right way to proceed, driving, idling, and buying?

In the highlands of the Sangre de Cristo Mountains between Santa Fe and Taos, we came to Truchas. Robert

Redford tried shooting *The Milagro Beanfield War* around Truchas and found he wasn't wanted—the only evidence of that disruption was a sign reading Milagro Gas.

A couple of hundred years ago, as the culture of Spanish New Mexico solidified into a class system, the poor mestizos and *genizaros* were encouraged to settle in outlier towns and serve as buffers against rapacious raiders like the Comanche, whose attacks had ensured the abandonment of the pueblo at Pecos. Truchas was one of those towns. Visits by priests were rare, and the isolated people evolved a sect of what I've heard called "morbid Christians."

Known as Penitentes, they spend Holy Week singing sorrowful hymns and enacting a repetition of Christ's death, a brother literally hauling a heavy cross to the hill on his back in order to suffer while others whip themselves bloody with knotted cords. Penitentes exist today much as they did, distant and proud. A writer I used to know was snooping around Truchas when he found himself faced by angry men wielding tire irons. They sent him right down the road. He said later, laughing as he spoke, "I completed my research in the New York Public Library."

Cruising down toward the Rio Grande, we imagined seeing landform patterns from O'Keeffe paintings on actual hills, and indulged a fantasy: an angular and aging, beautiful woman at her paintings on the roadside, a black Model A parked alongside, a slope folding into a gully which was then transmutated into an image which might be suggesting the beauties of women's so-called nether parts or simply remind us that translucent mysteries are part of one another. The idea of her lifetime's work was no longer boring.

Across the Rio Grande, we ascended to Los Alamos. The layout of life there looked planned, orderly, small-town streets, as the poet Richard Hugo said of another Western town, "laid out by the insane"—a community theater near a nuclear research facility; families poised beside the possibility of apocalypse. Lawns and incandescent closure.

On the morning of July 16, 1945, down on the southern New Mexico badlands called Jornada del Muerto, a device exploded that cast "the light of a thousand suns." The fireball grew to be shaped "like a monstrous, convoluting brain." Hard to think this is where it began.

Bandelier is an ancient native village site in a deep secluded canyon north of the plateau where those scientists live and work. Prehistoric inhabitants carved dwellings into the cliffs. Through centuries of travel they'd worn knee-deep paths into the soft stone. This, for me, spoke of human continuities and persistence as nothing I'd seen recently. This, I thought, is why I'm here, what I'm going to love about this neck of the woods. Then my automobile went to ailing— semiplugged emission-control system. We barely made it back up the hill to the plateau and Los Alamos.

Far away, as we chugged through the twilight, Santa Fe lighted the horizon and looked pretty sexy to escapees from ice-bound Montana. Annick and I ran through another late round of baked brie with lingonberries, laid up in a casita, and woke to warm springtime.

Many in the the modernist art movement before the First World War believed they might find a home in some local neighborhood. Many, not just artists, still do. Allegiance to a coherent local life-style might define us. Given a chance, in the proper setting, we might find that we were content in a class-less society, a free and forbearing interwoven culture. That was and is the echoing dream.

Intellectuals and artists began trying it out in utopian colonies like Carmel, Provincetown, and Woodstock. But homelands are cemented together by networks of story, as at Hopi and Zuni pueblos. True neighborhoods take a generation or so to evolve while grocers and schoolteachers and painters and poets and single mothers and buckaroo wives and Navajo medicine-men shop along the same streets, and argue out dif-ferences in the same cafés and city-council meetings. They aren't often created, they happen. Utopian colonies tend to be a cooked-up paradise for the like-minded.

The colony that developed in the Santa Fe/Taos area during the 1920s was inspired and orchestrated by Mabel Dodge Luhan, a monied idealist who came to New Mexico after years in Florence and Greenwich Village. Mabel found that the pure light across red-rock extrusions, timbered snow-topped moun-tain peaks behind them, combined with the "innocent" emo-tional honesty of the native people, formed an ideal physical and psychic setting for the new-age society she was determined see flower. In 1918 she built an adobe mansion on land near the Taos Pueblo, and took up with and eventually married Tony Luhan, a Taos Indian.

Intent on promoting her paradise, Mabel began inviting writers and artists to come share what she'd found. The list of those who took her up on the offer over the next decades is testimony to the power of her vision (and money): Carl Jung, Willa Cather, Leopold Stokowski, Edmund Wilson, Paul Strand, Ansel Adams, Edward Weston, Robinson Jeffers, Aldous Huxley, Martha Graham, Georgia O'Keeffe—and many, many others. Mabel put the famous people up, found them places of their own if they stayed on, and encouraged them to reflect on New Mexico in their work. I imagine her guests traveling dusty tracks over the deserts in rigid black 1920s touring cars.

D. H. Lawrence was initially entranced. "I have never experienced anything like New Mexico...the fierce, proud silence of the Rockies...the desert sweeping grey-blue...the pine-dotted foothills...What splendor!...Never is the light more pure and overweaning than there...In New Mexico the heart is sacrificed to the sun and the human being is left stark, heartless, but undauntedly religious."

But Lawrence was soon reminded that homes weren't so easily found. "It's all rather like a comic opera played with solemn intensity. All the wildness and wooliness and westernity and motor-cars and art and sage and savage are so mixed up, so incongruous, that it is a farce, and everybody knows it."

Lawrence moved on. Frieda, his widow, came back, to inter his ashes on the little mountainside ranch that Mabel had traded for the manuscript of *Sons and Lovers.* Frieda lived out her life in New Mexico.

Georgia O'Keeffe came to New Mexico in May 1929. She was forty-one years old and had once worked as a teacher in Amarillo on the Texas panhandle. An established painter, she was traveling without her husband, the enormously influential

Alfred Stieglitz, a New York gallery owner and modernist photographer, to spend a summer painting.

"No one told me it was like this," she told Mabel. O'Keeffe soon bought a Model A and was gone exploring. She remembered thinking, looking back on that first summer, "This is my world, but how to get into it." When time came to return to New York, she took with her a barrel of the bones she'd gathered from the desert. It was her habit to carry home pinecones and shells and weathered wood and feathers, mementos of a vitality which is both vividly surrealist and vanishing, vanishing, the core of emotion which emerges from her paintings. Which is hard to see until you forget about those god-awful framed posters.

In 1940 she bought a few acres and an adobe house at a dude outfit called Ghost Ranch, sixty miles west of Taos, and had exterior walls torn out, to be replaced with windows from which she could gaze out to a forested flat-topped butte, the Pedernal, and to yellow, red, and coral cliffs behind the house. In 1945 she bought a house overlooking the Chama River in the little nearby town of Abiquiu. After Stieglitz died, in 1946, she moved to New Mexico to stay. She died there, aged 98, in 1986. Her life and work stand of course for themselves, but also as a validation of Mabel Dodge Luhan's intentions, which otherwise went rather stale.

Mabel visualized an oasis culture in which to escape repressive racial, sexual, and religious bigotry, and to a great degree what she got was all that. But she allowed wealth and high living to stand as a barricade between herself and her friends who came to visit, and the invention of a "new society." What Mabel created, despite all her well-intended efforts, was a hide-out whose pleasures were there for the wealthy, and the well-connected, the artistically at least semi-talented, a society deeply concerned about style and manners. In the long run Mabel's new society had more to do with privilege than New Mexico or Indians in their enduring pueblos. Georgia O'Keeffe, in the end, seems like a happy accident.

Another run of accidents began in 1922 when a young man from the East, Robert Oppenheimer, took a pack trip into Frijoles Canyon (Bandelier). In 1937 Oppenheimer went back, and in 1942, when the United States was seeking to site the Manhattan Project, he proposed that the weapons laboratory be located at a school on a mesa north of Frijoles Canyon. The rest is Nagasaki, Hiroshima, ICBMs, public history.

As a direct result, the central New Mexican corridor, along the Rio Grande, is said have the highest percentage of Ph.D's of any population in the United States. Maybe that's true, maybe not—point is, it's plausible. Scientists continue to gather in and around Santa Fe and Los Alamos, for instance the Nobel Prize-winner Murray Gell-Mann, who discovered the quark. Brains like to hang out with brains; they enjoy feedback and strong conversation as they attempt to unravel mysteries. And according to George Johnson, in *Fire in the Mind: Science, Faith, and the Search for Order,* the mysteries under consideration lately, by a cadre of scientists in and around Santa Fe, are running at the highest possible level of likely irresolvable complexity.

- How could the universe arise from pure nothing?
- How does the hard-edged material world we experience arise from the indeterminacy of the quantum haze?
- How does life arise from the random jostling of dead molecules?
- How does the mind arise from the brain?

And the greatest mystery:
- Are there really laws governing the universe?

Or, is the order we see imposed by the prisms of our nervous systems a result of the way evolution wired our brains? Scientists don't like that idea. For scientists, Johnson says, belief in natural law is "a deep though seldom stated hypothesis. In a way, it is the basis for their religion."

The cutting-edge group in Santa Fe is trying to fathom how chaos resolves into repetitive symmetries in the processes of nature. But they continue to find irresolvable mystery. Johnson links them to Penitentes at Truchas in their *morada* celebrating Holy Week, and to pilgrims who stream along the narrow highways toward Chimayó, and to ceremonial dancers in the various Tewa pueblos, like San Ildefonso, along the Rio Grande.

Tribal peoples, Penitentes, and the scientists, cultures devoted to arcane knowledge and utter secrecy, resemble one another—humans responding to mysteries—who and what we are, where, and why? But the nature of things isn't likely to reveal its ultimate secrets. That's the oldest story, one we all know in our secretive hearts, told in so many forms. No answers. Not in this life. So we throng to versions of home.

"Santa Fe style" is a "look." It can be purchased in the form of silver and turquoise jewelry or homes with Saltillo tile floors, ceilings made with aspen vigas, and R. C. Gorman posters. That style has been attractive for three-quarters of a century, and defined much of life in Santa Fe and Taos, for the privileged and those who serve them.

Seen from the outside, Santa Fe and environs can seem like a play-culture marketplace dedicated to maintaining status, a sort of interactive pseudomuseum peddling bogus authenticity and second-rate commodified art, nice design but not in exactly close contact with existential realities. The best of that style is hip, cool, and draws monied tourists like honey.

And style, per se, isn't necessarily bogus. The Santa Fe style is based on the colors and look of the deserts, native arts, and Hispanic cooking. The Santa Fe building code encourages an imitation of the pueblo architecture, natural forms ordered so as to create a staging ground for sacred rituals. And Santa Fe, after all, like most anywhere, is a place where people are trying to feel at home, in family and community. Why not stay connected to the best of what's evolved locally?

Recently I spent some time fondling books in a first-rate used and rare bookstore just up the block from the square, not a pleasure that can be often found in the West. It's always engaging to beat around in Santa Fe if you've got some money in your pocket. There's terrific food, fine wines, museums, opera, and vividly smart people, many of them dedicated to good-hearted work. Santa Fe at its worst seems stylish, exclusive, and self-absorbed. But seen another way, life there also can obviously be easily in touch with serenities while thick with information, a sweet deal if you're not working for a living locally. Like any resort town, Santa Fe has a cold, hard-assed, and quite commercial side. No place to hang around with your hat in your hand. But then uptown New York and riverbank Paris are far more status-conscious and exclusive, and they can be enjoyed, and even admired, and learned from.

CHAPTER SEVEN

The Spin We're In

Repetitions and variations, call and response, as in the blues, seem to lately be the running theme of our travels in the Southwest. As in life.

In recent years, crossing out of Utah, Annick and I turn east and cross the headwaters of the Paria River. Ahead lies the watery grave of what was one of the most exquisite runs of landform on earth, the Glen Canyon of the Colorado—now so drowned under Lake Powell and so profoundly lost. What to say about glories most of us never saw and never will see except in photographs?

Wallace Stegner wrote of Glen Canyon this way: "When cut by streams, the Navajo sandstone, which is the country rock, forms monolithic cliffs with rounded rims. In straight stretches the cliffs tend to be sheer, on the curves undercut, especially in the narrow side canyons. I have measured a six-hundred-foot wall that was undercut a good five hundred feet—not a cliff at all but a musical shell for the multiplication of echoes."

Of side canyons he said, "Hundreds of feet deep, sometimes only a few yards wide, they wove into the rock so sinuously that all sky was shut off. The floors were smooth sand or rounded stone pavement or stone pools linked by stone gutters, and nearly every gulch ran, except in flood season, a thin clear stream. Silt pockets out of reach of flood were gardens of fern and redbud; every talus and rockslide gave footing to cottonwood and willow and single-leafed ash; ponded places were solid with watercress; maidenhair hung from the seepage cracks in the cliffs."

Reading that, I recall the writer of guidebooks I encountered as he headed into the canyon of the Paria River from Lee's Ferry, and wonder if it's still like that up there, if he was going home to beauty, like the scientists in Santa Fe, to an addictive regard for the repetitive but coherent complexities which emerge from chaos.

Ed Abbey was one of the last to go down Glen Canyon before the dam was completed. In *Desert Solitaire* he wrote, "I saw only part of it but enough to realize that here was an Eden, a portion of the earth's original paradise. To grasp the nature of the crime that was committed imagine the Taj Mahal or Chartres Cathedral buried in mud until only the spires remain visible."

Glen Canyon, Abbey wrote, "was a living thing, irreplaceable, which can never be recovered through any human agency." Oftentimes whimsical but on that occasion a furious empiricist, Abbey is profoundly missed in the Southwest. He was absolutely a *thing,* like Glen Canyon. And like the canyon, he's so recently dead.

Annick and I drove above "beaches" and houseboat marinas

on the shores of the reservoir called Lake Powell and down through cliffs and across the concrete teardrop which is the abominable Glen Canyon Dam. We wondered how deep the water was, how dense the reefs of silt, and if the intricate canyons would wash clean even if the dam were torn out, if they would be luminous at daybreak or irrevocably tarnished.

Exposure to ten thousand varieties of man-made entropy, the wrecking of phenomena like the remnants of ten-million-year-old sand dunes our genes tell us to regard as sublime, is an ongoing Southwestern experience these days, and this was more of the same. Do not, I tell myself, indulge in prolonged pouting. Transformations are real, process, verbs and not nouns. Canyons and species don't last forever. So I tell myself. But lately, that dance has been proceeding at warp speed.

Just south of the Glen Canyon Dam we came to the sprawling power-plant/tourist town called Page. I can't think of a way to speak my mind about Page without probably estranging the hard-working folk who make livings there. Page is a striking example of what I call the monkeyed-up world—spastically alive and breeding. But out-of-control growth, to paraphrase Abbey, is the ideology of the cancer cell.

There's Glen Canyon Dam, Lake Powell, and the transient flotsam of second-rate tourism, and there's a gigantic coal-fired power plant on the hill back of town which belches a twenty-four-hour-a-day misery of gray haze, detectable for hundreds of miles, into what were mystically clean skies. Our sweet frantic species is overweaningly heedless and heartbreakingly destructive in the name of socioeconomic progress. Will our children forgive us this wreckage?

Maybe I'm out of control. Are these anywhere close to primary considerations? In a steakhouse barroom just off the main drag in Page, I sat a couple of stools down from a fellow who looked like some sort of white-headed, blue-eyed angel from the deserts—clean and well-kempt, missing his front teeth, some sort of fanatic. Obsessional people gravitate to deserts, maybe just because the air is (or was) so clear and it's possible to see so far. Maybe clean air is a metaphor for psychic clarity.

This man's eyes shone as he studied me over his gin and tonic. "Well," he said in a grating sort of not-often-used voice, "have you got things straight?"

"Straight" is a kind of code word. Obsessives are determined to get things clear and straight. No Keatsian holding of two conflicting ideas in the mind at the same time for them.

"Not really," I said. "Like what?" I was thinking about gulping my own gin and tonic and getting out of there, hunting up another joint to drink in.

"Like gin." He smiled, lips tight but smiling. "Like this goddamned entropy."

Another thing about clarity—it encourages long views.

"Maybe so," I said. "It's what you get."

"I like it," he said. "No bullshit about it." We seemed to be in agreement.

"Tell you what," he said. "Buy me another drink and I'll shut up about philosophy."

So what the hell. I ordered us both another. "Now," he said, "let's you and me sit here and keep quiet. Pretty soon the sun will be going down and that will be one hell of a thing. Always is."

This was the other side of obsession. I keep wondering, do long views, across treeless and thinly populated landscapes, induce fatalism? Does isolation and distance lead us to focus on the fragility of our so-called dreams, the direction we've chosen to go. Is it possible to live without dreams? Would we want to? In any event, maybe we'd be better off if our dreams weren't so entirely, always, centered on fulfilling desire.

That fellow and I were taking pleasure in splendor as it was and not some other thing we thought it ought to be, just keeping quiet, sipping our drinks, studying the sunset out the barroom window. That blue-eyed man and I, strangers looking out a wide tavern window, we witnessed colors from orange to indigo to blue-white in faint drifts of cloud over the dark Vermilion Cliffs. We did not wish to avert our eyes. Or at least I didn't.

Much of what most of us ultimately yearn for—psychic freedom, contact with ineffable significance, dignity, escape— was there for a short moment. Taking comfort, we were comfortable with one another.

The next morning, with Page in our rear-view mirror, Annick and I drove into the heart of the long plateau which constitutes northern Arizona. It's tempting, undulating along on narrow asphalt, to freewheel at semi-ecstatic speeds. With Beethoven's "Archduke Trio" rising and sighing from the CD deck, we lifted and fell in synchronization with the energies of sadnesses and recovery, memory and regret, going on with life anyway. Coherences and rhythms come to us as pleasure.

About twenty-five miles south of Page, Highway 89 breaks through a deep cut in the knife-edged ridge of the Cedar Tree Hills to emerge high on the Echo Cliffs. Listening to cantatas by Johann Sebastian Bach, his weaving of counterpoint again reminding us that we are irrevocably sewn into the cloth of things, we pulled onto an overlook and got out, the CD deck still thrumming away. The landscape, west and far below, was slightly unreal, the undulating course of Marble Canyon cutting through House Rock Valley, the Vermilion Cliffs somber in the morning and the dark green of the forested Kaibab beyond, stratas that had lifted and fallen and turned sideways and upside down for millions of years, familiar but jarringly strange. Is it this we are seeking, complexities we can't be rejected by or escape? Is this the homeland?

Crossing northern Arizona, we were drifting and dreaming across flatland swales and washes, the San Francisco Peaks in the distance, cruising through horizontally striped badlands in shades of gray, black volcanic cones and sandstone bluffs on the route to Flagstaff, a college town on the Mogollon Rim where we watched an NFL playoff game in a jock tavern (the sacred 49ers lost to the dreaded Cowboys, a sign our culture was failing). Seeking solace, we drove down off the Mogollon Rim into the leafy depths of Oak Creek Canyon, to Sedona, taken by mystic devotees to be a center where energies gather, as I understand it, and influence the future.

We enjoyed a Merlot we couldn't really afford, and mesquite-fired lamb chops while a sliver of moon hung belly-down in the purple night. It was clear. We deserved any and all delux treatment. The Lux. So forget the Dallas Cowboys. We were in the land of those who seem to get away with lives focused on diet, exercise regimes, and long walks into the vortex.

In 1987 the University of Montana agreed that I should be given time off during the dark winter months. With little idea of what we were doing, except that we wanted to wake up to sunlight, write in the mornings, and play a little golf or hike in the afternoon, Annick and I found ourselves in the oldie-goldie retirement town called Green Valley, which is strung along I-15 about thirty-five miles south of Tucson, past the Titan ICBM Museum, on the way to Nogales. The golf and typing were what we'd imagined, and we had a fine time hiking among the white-barked sycamore in Madera Canyon, just to the east in the Santa Rita Mountains, but our time there was not an entire success. Soon, quite soon, we were restive and scanning the real estate-for-rent pages in the Tucson newspaper.

What was our problem? Did we lack the imagination to connect in a community where we didn't know anybody? Maybe, but it wasn't just us, it was also Green Valley. It wasn't so much the so many graying folks, most of whom, like us, were escaping winter in some northern state. Rather, it was that there wasn't anybody else.

There weren't any young people, or people of any color other than white, except for the hired help, there wasn't any-body on in-line skates in the mall, there were just retirees driving the streets in electric golf carts and sniffing can-taloupe at Safeway. But why so negative? Maybe I've lost my head. Or maybe, on the other hand, as Tom McGuane once wrote in another context, "it's one of the troubles we're having with our republic."

I'm talking about enclaves, oftentimes gated and guarded, of well-to-do people, in this case mostly white and elderly. Green Valley seemed to me to be an internment in which I nevertheless enjoyed the golf, a mortuary community.

But I'm being unfair. No doubt a spectrum of opinion about the responsible conduct of life was alive in Green Valley—pacifists, birders back from padding their lifetime lists in Costa Rica, hard-headed sue-the-bastards enviros and nuke-'em-all-into-the-stone-age racist warmongers and screw-everybody-I've-got-mine-in-a-Swiss-bank capitalists. Maybe an occasional revolutionary (however hard to spot).

But enclaves based on an institutionalized class distinction (money) usually turn out to be brain-dead versions of paradise, inhabited by people with nothing to discuss because they already know what they think, people who are threatened by other opinions. They've spent a lifetime accumulating the right to a few last insulated years. Nobody is going to take those years away. Not many such people are interested in rocking the boat. What often results is an emotionally frozen community, people interested in taking care of number one and staying as insulated as possible against perplexity.

Annick and I lucked out. We found another casita, this time inside the grounds at the Omni Tucson National Golf Resort and Spa, on Arnold Palmer Way, in a truly gated community. The price was for unfathomable reasons affordable, and we loved it. So wherein, if anywhere, lay the difference, if there was a difference?

Going to resorts is like crossing into another country, where it's supposedly easy to live according to the natural pace of the body. Sleep until noon, have a massage. Obey some inner child. Visit the hummingbirds out at the Arizona-Sonora Desert Museum as they negotiate the swift business of their lives. Or go hiking at daybreak, into the cholla-lit-by-sunrise epiphany. The Tucson National, despite gatekeepers, worked out like that for us. The patio behind our casita looked over an undulating, manicured fairway to the wide sandy course of the Cañada del Oro, which carried floodwaters down from the Santa Catalina Mountains during the monsoons of July. While other fairways ran on the far side, coyotes roamed along the Cañada in search of rabbits and poodles to devour. At dusk, deer and javelina came out from the brushy thickets. Roadrunners and lizards, rabbits, doves, and owls were around all day. Annick wandered the animal trails like a child seeking the unpredictable. Twilight was the secret time she loved best. But it was also the dangerous time, since the Cañada del Oro is a miles-long tract of wildness inside the city. She found, despite patrols by white-shirted security from the Tucson National, recently used transient camps. So men from security kept track of her comings and goings. But Annick paid them little attention and went on traipsing.

Off our patio there was a fine cottonwood leafing out for another spring, clamorous with an evolving population of blue grosbecks, mourning doves, and cardinals, green-tailed towhees and cactus wrens, four species of thrashers, and phainopepla, a vivid black creature which likes to feed on mistletoe (how it came to us we didn't know). I sat on that patio, waiting for

Annick to return from the Cañada del Oro, paying attention to the antics of songbirds and was content with just that.

And we were in a city, free to explore into the energies of the southside Hispanic community, which was exotic to me (Annick grew up near northside Chicago). Off Speedway, west of the interstate in Tucson, there's a café called Mariscos Chihuahua, which is a prime favorite with me. I love the seafood, and think of it as the happy café, where smartassed talk and laughing happens. I surreptitiously watched mommas and daddies and grandma and grandpa and young wide-eyed girls and little whispering boys and babies in arms. The light of their regard for one another lit up the walls. With little idea how those people had earned the money for their meal, or why they seemed so pleased with one another, I nevertheless fed off their energies; we were to the edges of the turista loop, seeing over into a neighborhood where we liked the look of things even if we didn't know what was involved in living there or of the sadnesses that touched those people. We were only with them, after all, when they were at dinner together and thus celebrating.

The next spring I taught at Arizona State University and we lived way out on the Beeline Highway, east beyond Phoenix in Fountain Hills, which was famous for the towering fountain of water which shot off at undetermined times over the man-made lake in the desert—an advertising gimmick. At the university, people looked at me curiously. Fountain Hills, I gathered, was not a cool move.

Annick fractured her ankle jumping off a boulder, but we wrote and I finally read Rilke, and we hiked the eventually flowering Sonoran Desert in undeveloped ravines, where, lately, a terrific golf course has been built. What to say? At twilight we gazed east over the spectacle of Red Mountain and on to the Superstitions and distant unsettled highlands where morning once or twice revealed light snow. People on our street, which was named after golfer Lee Trevino, were into double-income families, both parents in business suits as they commenced a commute. Their kids joined other kids walking to school. They were obviously trying to lead well-lighted, upscale lives. Where in hell was the problem?

Phoenix and Tucson and Albuquerque, with their stunning expenditures of nonrenewable energies, are like cities everywhere, complex in their particular ways but insulated like spaceships. In the Southwest, cities are not so much stuck in the past as intently dreaming up designer versions of an air-conditioned paradise centered on wealth, ease, and privilege. It's easy to fault them.

Privilege no doubt breeds selfishness, and tends to suppress generosity. Privileged enclaves are indeed one of the troubles we're having with our republic. But class distinctions are double-edged and cut various ways. It's important, if we're interested in fairness, to remember that people in those cities are confronting mortality, cherishing their progeny and friends, dancing and laughing and praying while often feeling as utterly lost as we do. Or, contrarily, as at home.

Nevertheless, a deeply anti-democratic culture seems to be forming in the Southwest. If money and power live isolated, chances of dissolving class distinctions are few. The problem, I guess, is within us, the old competitive animal, as we strive to solace and to better ourselves.

Annick and I encountered a Gila monster crossing the perfectly mown grass of an upscale fairway, the ancient creature scuttling toward cover in the bush. How had it, the stranger, so otherwise and alive, yet dangerous, poisonous, managed to survive? Mainly, I guess, by staying furtive.

In the 1960s, when he was living outside Cuba, New Mexico, Bill Eastlake befriended Ed Abbey (a pair to draw to, of naturals if ever there was one). They talked themselves in a grudge against billboards along the highway between Santa Fe and Albuquerque, and began traveling the road after midnight with chain saws in the back of a pickup. "Falling signs," Eastlake said. "It was foolproof. You could see headlights for twenty miles." Foolproof was something those boys liked.

So what's that possibly apocryphal story add up to beyond name-dropping? Maybe it's just about admiring the ways of a countrified world too much to give up without a fight.

John Graves, from the Texas plains north of the Brazos, wrote in *The Last Running* of a cowman who grew old as settlement came to the short-grass prairies. That man had seen the end of the bison culture and the ruination of the terrible Comanche, left helpless after their herd of fourteen hundred horses was shot by the U.S. Cavalry in Palo Duro Canyon, under the Cap Rock. Broken-hearted by the losses connected to preparing for death, Grave's story is not a whit softheaded. The old man says, "We had a world once." After that vote in favor of evolved ways, he shuts up. He lets it go at that.

It's common knowledge that life and work are often successfully conducted by free individuals operating in a communal fashion, each subsumed in collective projects. But collective
traditions and thinking that are understood to be inviolable, if
the community is to survive, can be smothering.

In *Dakota,* Kathleen Norris writes about towns on the
short-grass plains which have withered into emotional paralysis.
Unwilling to evolve, they're in fact offended by the possibility.
Change, Norris writes, "means failure."

Emotionally gridlocked communities are everywhere in
the Southwest, not just in retirement settlements. In long-
established backland towns, where extended families have lived
for generations, we see signs of prideful care—tight fences and
neat gardens above the creek, a couple of good saddle horses and
milk cows on lush meadows. But beyond occasional American
flags flying above immaculately white-painted houses, there's
no sign they want much to do with anything beyond the confines of their particular watershed.

In southern New Mexico, just south of Truth or
Consequences, Highway 152 leaves Interstate 25 and winds to
the west through the Mimbres Mountains toward the old open-
pit mining town of Silver City. It's a sweetheart drive; Emory
Pass is the sort of two-lane blacktop where advertising agencies
like to film sports cars negotiating turns at high speeds, asphalt
twisting up through evergreen forests, and then the falling
away to grasslands along the Mimbres River.

Silver City, at about six thousand feet in elevation, unlike
ranch communities in the mountain territory reaching off
north, seems to be opening out to the world. At dinner, writer

Sharman Apt Russell and her husband, Peter Russell—who works for the Nature Conservancy—explained that fresh halibut was a bright new luxury item in Silver City.

A long-time mining town, Silver City's economy is dominated by the Phelps Dodge Mining Company, and the three giant copper mines they operate. But the price of copper is less than half of what it was six years ago, and the company is closing one of its mines, dropping 650 jobs. That's big, bad news in Silver City.

But more important news, from a region-wide perspective, is recent wrangling over reclamation bonding for the mines. In 1993 New Mexico passed a mining law that demanded mines be reclaimed "to a condition that allows for the reestablishment of a self-sustaining ecosystem...appropriate for the life zone of the surrounding areas." Such work is very expensive. Cleaning up the Butte, Montana, district could cast 1.6 billion dollars. New Mexico asked Phelps Dodge to post a 759-million-dollar financial assurance bond for reclamation of its Chino mine, and it's expected that a similar bond will be required for its six-thousand-acre Tyrone mine. New Mexico was shocked. The Phelps Dodge counteroffer is 99 million dollars. Behind-closed-doors talks are proceeding. While no one in New Mexico wants to force the closure of those mines, the public recognizes they'll be picking up the tab if mining companies don't. And the costs are more than financial; they involve human health and an ecosystem semipermanently degraded by polluted groundwater.

An intense emotional and economic battle, traditional industries like mining and ranching and logging balanced against environmentalists, has of course been going on in the West for decades. Silver City happens to be the site for the latest episode.

It's a battle involving people who feel their traditional ways of making a living are being taken away from them by outsiders. Feelings run deep, and are sometimes quite irrationally furious. Locals feel attacked, and think of going to war. Should the so-called New Story of the so-called New West emphasize human home-lands and traditional ways of making a living, or ecological restora-tion? Implications are both psychic and practical. Stay tuned.

It's commonplace for outsiders to express disregard for peo-ple who live in the backlands. The real issue in negotiations with rural enclaves is often respect. A version of that story is being acted out in the hill country north and west of Silver City—reaches of grassland at nine thousand feet in elevation, aspen and cottonwoods along mountain creeks. Much of that sparsely inhabited territory is public land, owned by you and me, managed by the United States Forest Service. A lot of it has beyond question been overgrazed for decades, often to the detri-ment of threatened or endangered species. But local ranchers tend to regard it as theirs, by right of custom, to use as they have always used it.

Lately there's been a duel over restoration of those lands, particularly wetlands, between the ranchers and people who claim the ranchers have grazed their cattle irresponsibly. There's serious hostility.

After my evening in Silver City, I stopped at Uncle Bill's Bar in Reserve, about a hundred miles north, which has been called "the statehouse of redneck anger." A hardhanded old fel-low at the bar studied me when I came in.

"There's the boy I'm going to have unload my hay," he said, laughing, talking loud and about me. I was out the door.

But despite anger, the ranchers, predictably, lost their battle with the environmentalists. The Forest Service has reduced grazing allotments.

The ranchers have responded by saying they are being driven out of business. And probably some of them are. "In one year we'll be out of here," says Glen McCarty, whose family has ranched northwest of Reserve since 1884. They're being asked to live at a subsistence level. And nobody wants to live at a subsistence level.

And, as with many country people, not just in the hills of New Mexico, there's a feeling that promises are being broken. This is America, which said, "give me your poor, your homeless." After enclosures in Scotland and starvations in Ireland, peasants crossed the Atlantic to the American South, and their descendants came to eastern Texas and Arkansas, and some of their descendants came to the beautiful isolated hills of western New Mexico, where they would never be crowded or dispossessed. Now, after four or five generations, look what's happening again.

It's increasingly common knowledge that killing off species, unto extinction, is international insanity. What about rural communities? Aren't they, like urban neighborhoods, part of the glue that holds American identity intact? Driving them to poverty and belief in their own inconsequence, down a road toward essential extinction—on the short-grass prairies along the 100th meridian, or in the Mississippi Delta, or in New Mexico hills—is a manifestation of national irresponsibility.

The average per capita subsidy to agriculture in the European union is ten times that of the United States. And the majority of American subsidies go to corporate agriculture. If it seems important that we maintain responsible, educated social coherency in rural America, if we want a nation that is genuinely inhabited in all its parts, not just metroplexes hooked together by freeways and airlines, we might find ways to give social, economic, and ecological support to small ranchers in the hills of New Mexico. We could institute a system in which the nation pays farmers and ranchers for ecological restoration, good money for closely monitored performance, nothing given away. There are lots of problems to that notion. But we could work them through.

If our national leaders are interested in preserving ranchland communities, they might study some ideas being tried in the western bootheel of New Mexico. The 321,000-acre Gray Ranch was sold to the Nature Conservancy, for a rumored 18 million dollars, in 1990, and placed under easements which prevented it from being subdivided. In response, a group of local ranchers, fearful the Gray Ranch would become an open-to-the-public national monument (which they saw as an erosion of independent rural life), and that they would be forced to sell, and that ranchland would then be subdivided, formed what they called the Malpai Borderlands Group. Their purpose was to restore and maintain "the natural processes that create and protect a healthy, unfragmented landscape to support a diverse, flourishing community of human, plant and animal life in our Borderlands Region." Their primary strategy involved finding common grounds shared by ranchers, environmentalists, and government agencies.

Drummond Hadley, a poet, onetime pal of Gary Snyder's, and an heir to the Anheuser-Busch fortune, had fallen in love with cowboying and the desert country, and was ranching nearby. Hadley and his family formed the Animas Foundation, which bought the Gray Ranch, intending to "preserve, heal, restore and sustain wildlands and waters, their inhabitants and cultures." They began by restricting grazing, and with fires, both natural and set, burning off the weed species infesting severely overgrazed local ecosystems. Rested and burned, the old grasslands began coming back.

Hadley then thought of the "grassbank." If local ranchers were short of feed they could move cattle onto the Gray Ranch, where there was now plenty of grass. The value of that feed would be computed, and the ranchers would pay their bill by putting an equally valued portion of land into an easement which prohibited future subdivision. The Malpai Borderlands Group would raise money from donors and pay back the "bank" at the Animas Foundation. It's a system that could work. The elements that are involved include a willingness on the part of participants to undergo frustrating transactions, trust, and a source of funding. That source, if the grassbank notion is ever going to come into widespread use, will most likely be local and federal governments, i.e., us, the taxpayers.

Would those monies be paid back, ever? The answer, based on the century-long example of dozens of federally funded reclamation districts around the West, with hundreds of thousands of acres of managed wetlands and thousands of irrigators, is not likely, certainly not entirely. And trust is a workable notion in the community of the like-minded the Animas

Foundation deals with, but it's wispy basis for negotiation in the bottom-line world.

Some people, nevertheless, think federal money should back up the grassbanks. Losses could be written off as gifts the nation makes to itself, as with reclamation districts, or when we covered for defunct savings-and-loan institutions. They say preserving rural communities is as important as subsidizing United Airlines or Chrysler.

Unfortunately for ranchers, the range livestock industry is not widely understood as necessary. It's commonly thought federal funding for programs like the grassbank would constitute a handout. And to an industry with a long history of environmental destruction, an industry the nation doesn't need except in cowhand dreams. Loans, public will tends to think, should be secured, and foreclosures should always be a possibility.

Many environmentalists think it would be more sensible to simply retire federal and state lands traditionally used for grazing. Citizens with no connection to ranching are bidding on government grazing leases, which have by custom been the virtual private property of ranchers. And they are outbidding ranchers, who for generations have paid fees so low as to constitute a subsidy. In a case argued by the Arizona Center for Law in the Public Interest on behalf of a group called Forest Guardians, the Arizona Supreme Court slapped down state officials who claimed the leases were for grazers and no one else, saying the leases should be given to the "best bidder" even though the intent was to restore the land rather than run livestock. The land, say the environmentalists, is worth more to the nation than ranchers are likely to be capable of paying.

Another model for managing the relationship between public lands and ranching is evolving in New Mexico, in the Valles Caldera, or Valle Grande, a 95,000-acre reach of high meadowland under the timbered rim created when an ancient volcano collapsed. In mountains west of Los Alamos, on the headwaters of the Jemez River, the Valle Grande was a Spanish land grant known as the Baca Ranch. Most recently it was owned and lovingly maintained by a Texas oil family.

It's now public land, purchased by Congress in 2000, for 101 million dollars, and officially known as the Valles Caldera National Preserve. It won't be managed by federal agencies, but rather by nine trustees, led by a local named William deBuys, a writer. Their mission is to "protect and preserve the scenic, geological, watershed, fish, wildlife, historic, cultural and recreational values of the preserve, and to provide for multiple use and sustained yield of renewable resources within the preserve." Quite a mouthful, considering that they must also maintain the property as a working cattle ranch and attempt to be financially self-sufficient by 2017.

The board is presently committed to a limited elk hunting season in 2002, and a few hundred acres of timber thinning. But there will be, deBuys says, no elitist privileges, and the resources will be carefully maintained, while programs for all the people of New Mexico are slowly developed.

The following, from a book deBuys co-wrote with Alex Harris, called *River of Traps: A Village Life,* is testimony to respect for traditional Hispanic ways. "No barbed wire. Open fields. No Forest Service in the mountains with limits and regulations. Every man a farmer and rancher like every other.

Every woman, like every other, making do with what her family's fields and animals yielded. What you did not own you might freely borrow. Neighbors charged no rent. There was no *envidia,* say the old-timers. No envy. And almost no cash. If there was not always sufficiency, there was at least equality."

Mutual respect and trust. Sounds like a lost version of communal paradise. In *River of Traps,* an old man, lying on the ground beside an irrigation ditch, sleeping, in answer to fears that he might be dead says, "Yah, maybe so. But only like a cat, trying it out." Limited resurrections are possible.

Care and reverence loom large in William deBuys's marching orders. But environmentalists would like to forget the hunting, and get rid of the cattle on the Valles Caldera National Preserve. Some say they'd like to lock the gates.

Public will to preserve ranching based on public lands will only coalesce if preserving both ranchers and ecologies seems simultaneously possible and in the national interest. People say, shaking their heads sadly, maybe it's time for the range livestock industry to just wither away. They're quite willing to write off the sadness of the people whose sense of themselves is doing the withering. They look into the distance when I ask about funding health care, schools, and humanitarian aid for the poor in Mexico.

The Chiricahua Mountains, where the Apache held out against the U.S. Army until Geronimo surrendered for the last time in 1886, are topped with whimsically eroded stacks and towers of soft reddish rhyolite (people see figures in them, as they do in clouds, camels, forefingers pointing to heaven—one is called Duck on a Rock). Annick and I rove the twisting, graded gravel road over the eastern flank of the mountains, in and out of a scattered roadside settlement called Paradise, and into Cave Creek Canyon. Orangish stone walls rose into the sunset and white-barked sycamores existed like ghosts in shade along the Portal Creek. Portal, just down the road, is reputed to be half Ph.D's, mostly in the biological sciences. It's a birder's semisecret heaven.

But Douglas, a hundred miles south on the U.S./Mexican border, where the copper ore from Bisbee was processed before the mines closed, is *not* any sort of heaven. We checked out the art deco lobby in the Gadsden Hotel (spectacular, but the upstairs is indifferent at best; the beds, when we tested them, before moving on, were terrible). The old Vaquero Southwest, on the other hand, was still alive and taking tequila downstairs in the Saddle & Spur Tavern. Ranchland transactions were being resolved in a mixture of Spanish and English. The Saddle & Spur is a zone of transition. Tourist and cowhand versions of value, Anglo and Mexican, intersecting.

After appropriate margaritas, we drove on a half hour to the old Copper Queen Hotel in Bisbee, a hill-slope mining town inhabited by miners and their widows and artsy drifters. On weekends expect a party that can make its way into the streets. Bisbee gets it on. But I've lived beyond such delights. In the morning I stood on the porch and thought back to that long-ago night with Abbey and Peacock and Eastlake, saying goodbye to Bill Eastlake for the last time, and tried to imagine the boy I might have been if my grandfather had been old enough to go down in the Butte mines and not become a blacksmith for COPCO in Klamath Falls.

By noon, after dallying with hummingbirds in Ramsey Canyon, another paradise for birders, we made it to Nogales and crossed the border into Mexico in time to watched a white-haired Utah couple, seemingly sane, dicker over the price of a giant ceramic model of E.T. Then we drifted along into a high-end store called the Green Frog, where nobody would dicker on the prices for elegant, extravagantly imagined pottery. Annick spent serious money on plates to hang on her kitchen wall in Montana.

For unknown but undoubtedly awful reasons, on the streets we were beset by beggars. Mexico, we think, and its tragedies. We shrug them off as inevitable. But they're the result of economic policies. Dealings on the border have been, more than ever, inhumanely commodified since NAFTA, the North American Free Trade Agreement—an executive agreement— "opened" the border, at least to many economic transactions. It's proposed that it be almost entirely opened. But that's not likely; citizens across the Southwest are infuriated and terrified by the idea of their towns and economies being overwhelmed by thousands upon thousands, maybe millions, of immigrants.

In any event, a lot of goods cross without paying tariffs. So both economies benefit; that's the theory. And they perhaps have. But it hasn't been an entirely win-win deal. Good jobs in the United States were moved to Mexico, to be taken by workers earning less than minimum wage.

CEOs in the United States, interested in locating production facilities where wages are cheap and environmental constraints are not a serious factor, began setting up factories in borderland Mexico, directly connected to U.S. highways, rather than across the expensive seas in Malaysia. General Motors closed plants in the U.S. and Canada and became the largest employer in Mexico. Factories in Mexico, called *maquiladoras,* paint Fords, make steering wheels, brake shoes, entire Volkswagons, toasters, Sony TVs, ATMs, modems, you name it, and shorten their workers' lives by regarding environmental heedlessness as a part of doing business.

Thousands of Mexican citizens have moved north to the border in order to work in the maquiladoras, and trucks bearing "goods" produced with cheap Mexican labor enter the United States by the thousands every day. It's a system in which international corporations, and their customers, exploit the poor. In my own case, ducking away from the beggars in Nogales is typical of my relationship to the Mexican poor; ultimately it's much like a dealing between a master and slaves.

Meanwhile, the Mexican economy is driven by a "shadow market" in cocaine, heroin, medicines, pesticides banned in the United States, cowboy boots made of endangered sea-turtle flippers, and laundered money. The cocaine trade, it's said, is worth twice the profits of the Mexican petroleum industry. The police in Sinaloa province, along the western border, are said to cooperate with the drug dealers; they are not simply corrupt, they are in fact another batch of criminals. Mexico goes increasingly outlaw as a result of pandering to U.S. appetites. And hundreds of thousands migrate, or attempt to migrate, into the U.S. The most lucrative racket, after dealing drugs and laundering money, is forging U.S. visas. It's claimed that 60 percent of the retail economy in Douglas and Nogales turns on drugs, and 25 percent of the economy in Tucson. The war on drugs, if it were to succeed, might destroy the economy in Mexico (not to speak of Tucson).

Eight hundred thousand Mexicans cross the border legally, many daily, some flashing plastic cards, which constitute a visa. Some have seasonal jobs; others go shopping at Wal-Mart (the Wal-Mart in Laredo, Texas, has the highest per square foot sales of any in the world; Wal-Mart's sales equal the total GNP of the world's ninety-three smallest national economies). They take jobs nobody else wants, then they go home to sleep in Mexico. That's fine with everybody at U.S. immigration.

But there are many who don't qualify for visas. They are poor and uneducated, often from the villages. They have no economic ties to anyone but a family which they can better serve by sending money from the U.S. They're seen as bad risks to overstay any kind of visa, and are semiautomatically rejected. Most don't bother to apply.

Four or five thousand are caught trying to cross the border illegally every twenty-four hours. Around Douglas, the hottest point for attempted entry, in March 1999, Border Patrol agents arrested 61,000—almost one hundred per hour.

But thousands of those who try the border each night succeed. They travel north to work as fruit pickers, gardeners and motel maids and domestic servants, ranch hands and garbage men. They, again, are not really a problem. They work at jobs nobody else wants, for less than a minimum wage, and maintain a very low profile. Lots of Americans love to hire them.

But we're troubled by those who fail. They haunt us, sad, eager people who hire a "coyote" to smuggle them across the border in the heat of summer and perish while locked in the trunk of an automobile or wander unto death without water in 120-degree heat. Pulsing needs and yearnings drive them and some die trying.

Our answer to the "problem" of illegal immigrants, like our answer to that other problem driven by desire, our exploding use of drugs, is a "war." The battle against illegal immigrants, just like the war on drugs, is against a tide that's not likely to subside in the foreseeable future. It's obviously an ongoing, expensive failure—militaristic, inhumane, and foolish.

Street theory has it that illegals, like the flow of drugs, constitute an unsolvable problem. But that's nonsensical. Long-term humane solutions don't lie with "wars" or trickle-down NAFTA economics. Responsible ways of dealing with our borderland troubles, to succeed, must center on *giving,* by both the U.S. and Mexican governments, and by international corporations which buy and sell on both sides of the border— cutting the poor in on the economic action.

National governments and the corporations could institute a system of long-term economic stimulus and social aid aimed directly toward the disenfranchised in urban ghettos and back-land villages. But there'd be no quick fixes; there'd be literally millions of attempts at graft, many of which succeeded; it would take generations and big-time funding.

Ethical morale among the Mexican public, and democratic control of both the Mexican government and international economic ties, might eventually evolve. Mexican citizens might generate the will to clean up their banking and justice system, and to put the lid on institutionalized graft. Mexico might become the good clean-handed, clear-hearted neighbor. It's not a clear choice, but it's our choice. Otherwise, we're looking at social and moral chaos. The world can't be bullied into order.

Conditions along the border are already out of control. I've been studying horrific pictures taken by street photographers and collected in *Juárez: The Laboratory of our Future*, with text by Charles Bowden, an introduction by Noam Chomsky, and an afterword Eduardo Galeano (whose three-volume *Memories of Fire* is the most necessary text for anyone interested in the underside of history in the Americas). "The precarious equilibrium of the world," Galeano writes, "which teeters on the brink of the abyss, depends on the perpetuation of injustice. The misery of the many makes possible the extravagance of the few."

There are photographs of desiccated bodies, many of them, the murdered, people involved in drug deals gone wrong, women who were raped and killed, shallow graves dug in the sand and uncovered by the wind. There are children harvesting the city dumps, contesting with dogs and goats for what food they can find. In *Juárez*, Charles Bowden writes, "you cannot sustain hope." I'm driven, eyeing those photos, to nausea. Sneaking glances, I see why so many are so frantic to escape the "Third World." Why so many, worldwide, are so furious when we exclude them from the "First World" party. Then I look away, as we mostly do. The book protests horrifying realities, and a future we're likely to have—the privileged alone in a set of increasingly isolated, barricaded enclaves spotted around the world; the poor wandering furiously in denuded homelands, plotting revenge.

A man at a party said, "Once we needed immigrants, we welcomed them. Now we don't need them, so we wall them out, and call them barbarians. One of these days, like they did to Rome, they're going to come after us."

In *An Empire Wilderness: Travels into America's Future,* Robert D. Kaplan says the border between the United States and Mexico is presently set up to function like the Great Wall of China, which never worked to save China. He also says that the border between the "Third World" and the "First" lies at the break between flatland barrios in south Tucson and the bajada foothills to the north, backed up against the Santa Catalina Mountains, where the privileged Hispanic and Anglos live. The disadvantaged looking north, and up, to a hated ruling class that's looking south, and down.

Tucson began a desert trading center, Spanish, Mexican, and Indian, hardhanded and dusty. Culture and amenities came to Tucson with the University of Arizona, and with immigrants from the east and north, monied retirees seeking refuge from winter or a cure for tuberculosis. Developers and elegant places to stay followed and flourished. The Arizona Inn, one of my favorites, was built during the Great Depression—breakfast by the pool, card games in the shade once the table has been cleared.

Tucson, these days, is several cities. One's in the barrios. Another is an underwatered tourist-and-retiree oasis up for grabs, ruled by developers who lay down mall after mall, and subdivision after high- and low-end subdivision, people devoted to the creation of wealth and not beauty. Another lies inside the gated, monied, retiree-tourist hideouts, where people want to be left to enjoy themselves among their own kind.

First-string tourist havens have developed on the high north side. La Paloma is open-passage architecture and swim-up-to-the bar-for-another-margarita pools, a Southwestern version of what must have been going in the minds of those Arab princes in Granada who created the Alhambra. Kids are whooping on the waterslide and adults wear Rolex watches while slowly swimming laps. For dinner, we crossed the parking lot to Janos, widely regarded as the finest eating establishment in Tucson. The menu was described as French-inspired Southwestern. A Spring Tasting Menu (five courses with wine) featured sea scallops marinated in citrus, honey, and mint, pan-seared and served on fruit salad with kiwi-and-mango coulis, citrus beurre blanc, salmon cavier, and a touch of avocado mousse. I ordered green-tea smoked duck, stir-fried bok choy, and spiced plums off the regular menu. When we retired to the lobby bar for a nightcup and dessert, a pianist played "Smoke Gets In Your Eyes" and "String of Pearls." This is indeed the life if you just blew in from Missoula in January.

The Lodge at Ventana Canyon has forty-nine suites and privacy is absolute. Guests are quiet and intent on sensible pleasures. It would not be the place to go alone unless you enjoy talking to yourself. For dinner we went up the hill to Loew's Ventana Canyon Resort. For openers we tried the pan-seared fois gras on challah toast, with kumquat compote, accompanied by a glass of *eiswein,* Sichel, Rheinpfalz, 1994. My main course was chilled Maine lobster with oven-dried tomatoes, tart apples and sweet corn under a lemon-basil vinaigrette. All gods, except those of fairness, were secure in their heavens. Blue butterflies, the next morning, flitted among cactus in the rough.

At the Omni Tucson National, strung along that desert wash, ducks feed in a pond by the ninth green. Great horned owls call from the cottonwood trees. A massage with hot stones in the spa turned me hallucinatory with pleasure. Hard to imagine what women endure, with the herbal wraps, wax treatments, and facials. Annick emerged glowing and limber in body and mind. Folks in the Legends Sports Bar watched the Lakers on TV and smoked Cuban cigars they'd brought with them.

For upscale shopping, check out the boutiques in St. Phillips Square. Have lunch at Cafe Terra Cota. Or wander the old downtown and for lunch go to the Cafe Poca Cosa. Suzana Avila re-creates her menu of vivid borderlands food daily. Order the mole, whatever flavor, and hope the corn tamale soufflé will be on today's menu.

In *An Empire Wilderness,* Kaplan finds almost no urban planning in Tucson; neighborhoods don't last long enough for communal ties to develop; Tucson is a city in transit, where stress indicators—single motherhood, juvenile crime—are all up. The Southwest is full of "low-wage one-story encampments with a high proportion of drifters and broken families."

The neighborhoods that most interest Kaplan are the barrios, more border towns, governed if at all by the loyalties and authority of seventy-five known gangs. A retired policeman tells him of drive-by shootings and crack houses, kids turning into "monsters." Kaplan says, "Tucson is becoming several garrisons, where each house is more isolated than ever before."

Kaplan asked a former gang leader, "What's a gang?" The man said, "A gang enforces order from chaos. A gang is about pride and respect." He went on to say, "I know almost nobody in south Tucson who has bought into America."

Spend enough time braving out isolations and you may find you're losing contact with what self you ever had, and not ever at ease, that you're forgetting why you should care about anything or body other than yourself, and wondering why not find some hideaway and give up on the worrying and fussing. In *Blues for Cannibals,* Charles Bowden quotes Jeremiah 12:11-12:

> *They have made it a desolation;*
> *desolate, it mourns me.*
> *The whole land is made desolate,*
> *but no man lays it to heart.*
> *Upon all the bare heights in the desert*
> *destroyers have come....*

Bowden tells of a hideout which he says "is nowhere. These people look to be trash. Dopers. Welfare bums, junkies, tax dodgers, traffic violators. Gun nuts." Hideaways have been vanishing, he says, under golf courses and subdivisions. "But now they are coming back, sprouting up in the heart of our great cities, festering along the romaniticized blue highways." They are the homes "of those who endure but do not endorse...." The estranged in nests, where the insulted go, where the contest for power and acquisitions is understood as fundamentally without meaning. Homelands for those who refuse, Bartelby and Melville. I knew a horseman on the eastern

Oregon deserts who said that after a few weeks in the outback "you don't care what they're doing in town. Town is a fucking disease." Like heartbreak.

Jimmy Santiago Baca, born in 1952, is a poet, essayist, playwright, and screenwriter. In 1987 he won the American Book Award for his poetry; in 1992 he co-produced *Bound by Honor*, a feature film about gang culture in East Los Angeles and violent race relations among prisoners in California's federal prisons.

Baca grew up poor, first in a backlands New Mexico town called Estancia, then in Albuquerque. By thirteen he was in a detention center. In his recent memoir, *A Place to Stand: The Making of a Poet*, Baca writes, "After being stripped of everything, all these kids had left was pride—a pride that was distorted, maimed, twisted, and turned against them, a defiant pride that did not allow them to admit that they were human beings and had been hurt." As a teenager "we'd get high, cruise around, maybe get in a fight." He saw "the narrowing of life's possibilities in the cold, challenging eyes of the homeboys in the detention center; you could see the numbness in their hearts...All of them had been wounded, hurt, abused, ignored; already aggression was in their talk...each of them knew they could be hurt again..."

Baca ended up in prison, in solitary confinement, finding solace in memory. "Stretched out flat on my back, arms covering my eyes, I would replay events over and over again like a sexual fantasy.

"I went on like this for weeks, reliving the fable of my life, rediscovering from my isolation cell the boy I was and the life I'd lived." Remembering his childhood in Estancia was like recalling paradise, his grandfather carrying "me back home under the stars and moon on his shoulders."

In "Martin" he writes,

> A voice in me soft as linen
> unfolded on midnight air,
> to wipe my loneliness away—the voice blew open
> like a white handkerchief in the night
> embroidered with red roses,
> waving and waving from a dark window
> at some lover who never returned.

And so, thus, reimagining the story which defined his losses, learning to retell it to himself precisely, he began the process of reinventing his chances in terms of his emotional homeland, that which was most beloved. As I see it anyway; I have no idea what Jimmy Santiago Baca would think of my reaction. As he must know, the work goes out; strangers use it for their own purposes. Baca gives me heart.

The fertile valley of the Rio Yaqui, once known as Mexico's Breadbasket, one of the most fertile regions in Mexico, on the Sea of Cortes south of Guaymas, is the homeland of Yaqui Indians, who grew and bred locally adapted crops, including wheat called White Sonora, introduced in the 1690s by missionaries. In recent years, however, the valley has been seriously degraded by the Green Revolution in agriculture. In both environmental and social ways.

An agricultural scientist named Norman Borlaug won the Nobel Prize for developing a widely adaptable, highly productive hybrid wheat fueled by large doses of fertilizer, pesticides, and herbicides. The soil, a wiseass said, was only there to keep the plants from falling over sideways. Between 1950 and 1990, thanks to hybrids and the 250 pounds of nitrogen fertilizer added to each acre of floodplain soil, wheat yields in the Yaqui Valley increased four-fold. But another result of the Green Revolution was groundwaters and soils contaminated by heavy chemical use.

The cost of fertilizer is now a quarter of the cost of producing a crop; toxic pesticides, some applied forty-five times during the growing season, affect the health of farmworkers, and workers are chronically underpaid. Like so many of the poorest of the poor from all over Mexico, they are joining the migration north, to fields and orchards in the United States. The ongoing saga of NAFTA: agribusiness imports chemicals from the United States; Mexico deports citizens.

But this is not altogether a story about defeat. Guadalupe is a part of Phoenix, forty acres situated on an unwatered southside knoll, where dislocated Yaqui acquired the right to settle, and many have lived for generations. What sings to me at Guadalupe is bicultural religion (native and Catholic) which I take to be of universal validity, and the intensity of the ceremonies in which they celebrate it. A young stranger, on a cold night at one of their ceremonies, a girl with swirling red and green tattoos, holding a can of Coors, looked at me sort of wild-eyed and said, "These fucking people believe in something beautiful."

The Yaqui believe their ancestors are alive in a mythological "tree world," the *huya ania,* a version of the fertile Rio Yaqui Valley. In that world all creatures, including rocks and water, are alive in community, and converse with one another in a universal language, which is song. The Yaqui believe their ancestors, like those of the Australian Aborigines, defined their world while singing it into being.

They also believe in another world, the *sea ania,* a flower world, which is the *huya ania* as it blooms, a mirror of the Rio Yaqui bottomlands in blossom. Flowers are metaphors for all that is good and beautiful, and stand for grace flowing down to us from heaven.

Among the ancient Yaqui songs are deer songs, in the voice of the little brother deer, which remind the Yaqui of the continued existence of the magical worlds which mirror the world in which they live. At ceremonies three men sing while a deer dancer, who embodies the spirit of the deer, which comes from the flower world, acts out the drama, an elaborate costumed version of the Christian myth learned centuries ago from Jesuits. Young boys, under vow to the Blessed Virgin, dressed like the Virgin in long skirts and embroidered blouses, wearing crowns made of cane and brightly colored streamers, dance to violin and guitar music. After the crucifixion and agony, after enactments in which evil forces attempt to capture the church, good triumphs, defeating evil with music, prayers, and flowers, and the young boys dance finally around a Maypole. The Yaqui believe that the blood of Jesus as it fell from the cross mingled with the earth and was miraculously transformed into flowers that filled heaven and the earth. Flowers are the reward.

The Yaqui also perform a "deer killing" ceremony, which releases the spirit of the dead from confinement on "this weeping earth." The deer dancers and the deer singers are joined by the *pahkolam* or "old men of the festival," who are stripped to the waist and wear small wooden masks as they mime, dance, and joke with one another and the crowd. Their clowning and "games" are rude and an often hilarious commentary on Yaqui society and the world at large, and counterpoint the dignity of the deer dancer. They pursue and kill the deer, singing as they do but jumbling the words and rhythms, their foolishness contrasting to the killing itself. The deer song finishes,

> *I become enchanted.*
> *My enchanted body is glistening,*
> *sitting out there.*

The deer, after the dance, is laid on a bower of branches and skinned. It is miraculously transformed into a "flower" and reborn into the wilderness world, representing the deer who have died so humans can live.

A year ago, going south, we drove south from Las Vegas through Wickenburg and a vivid sunset over the Joshua tree desert, into the west-side outskirts of Phoenix at nightfall.

Though we'd once lived four months in Phoenix, the interior expressways were numbered and construed in ways that soon had us lost in a doomed looping-along-at-seventy-miles-an-hour-in-the-night sci-fi dream. We circled into the abstractions of the mod-pod airport, through unloading areas, and far out to the fringes of the Maricopa Indian Reservation before returning to finally escape into Tempe. That traveling was hell for the privileged.

While driving the metroplex, even for people like us, sometimes hypnotized by the flow in our insulated CD-deck, air-conditioned way, it's ordinary to complain that we're feeling on the verge of being overwhelmed. Driving, and it's necessary to drive if you want to get anywhere—there's not much in the way of public transportation— begins to seem like a virtual activity. Traffic moves at paces not suited to the human nervous system. Travelers find they're receiving way too many stimuli to process. This results in failures of nerve and purpose, psychic fibrillation.

E. B. White once wrote, "Everything in life is somewhere else, and you get there in a car." Sure seems true in Phoenix, where car culture is semi-absolute. Hard to find a serious bookstore, but no problem if you need hubcaps

An editor who grew up there described Phoenix as "a hundred square miles of kitty litter." It was an expression of disgust by a man who seemed to loath the city that circumstances intended as his homeland, an ordinary reaction among people who've come of age feeling trapped and bored.

Phoenix is part of a worldwide phenomena. Urban populations are exploding. Half our global population—2.85 billion people—live in urban centers at present. More than 90 percent of 2.05 billion people who are expected to be added to the world's population over the next thirty years will be located in metroplexes. The "Third World" is only 150 miles south of Phoenix, and coming north. Count on it.

What's happening in Phoenix is easy to understand. This is the West, this is America, and we're individuals. Sure, we like to travel alone. We own cars and garden homes, and that makes us independent. That's what Westerners tend to think. Thomas Jefferson would be proud of us. One wonders.

In 1956 Dwight Eisenhower signed the Federal-Aid Highway/Interstate Highway Act to create the National System of Interstate and Defense Highways. Our national frenzy of freeway building began. Between 1977 and 1995 U.S. governments spent barely 14 percent of their transportation budgets on mass transit and Amtrak; the balance went for roads and highways. The British and French, on the other hand, ordinarily spend 40 to 60 percent of their transportation budgets on mass transit and rail. An unintended result of the Interstate Highway Act has been the explosion of expressway systems within cities (36 percent of all federally aided–highway miles are in urban areas). There's twice the roadway in New York City as there is in London, five times as much as in Paris. It's my guess Phoenix would rank way out off the end of the chart, even though public transportation doesn't cost any more than expressways.

Integrated neighborhoods have withered, insulating social and economic classes from one another, into posh upscale suburbs and economically depressed slums and barrios around dying inner cities. Any sense of inhabiting a cherished home-land fragments. Ultimately, moral paralysis sets in, a death of belief that any form of responsibility, like justice in our society, is one of our concerns. Look away, look away.

It's argued that cities like Phoenix haven't yet generated what most of us yearn for in terms of community—spaces organized on a human scale, where people walk and mingle, moving at speeds our interior animal, the old walking creature, is psychically equipped to find comfortable. But designers argue otherwise. They say neighborhoods exist in the malls.

There are three basic contemporary city planning models. There is the traditional, as in Paris, old neighborhoods con-nected by streets, buses, and subways. There is also the Manhattan model, the grid, each block and skyscraper its own island (except that Manhattan is of course patterned with clas-sical neighborhoods and wouldn't be livable otherwise). And there is the Las Vegas model, explored in *Learning From Las Vegas* by Robert Venturi, Denise Scott Brown, and Steven Izenour (1972). Malls and strip development were proposed as unifying urban locations. The most favored activity is shop-ping—the utterly commodified marketplace proposed as psy-chically organizing. It's a model Southwestern cities have bought into. Phoenix has a run of bright upscale malls, like the Borgata and El Pedregal Festival Marketplace at the Boulders, and the Biltmore Center. They're places where I'm inclined to be ashamed of my shirt. But who's looking at me? Nobody.

Nobody, for the most part, is looking at anybody. They're looking at decor, and the ways people have decorat-ed themselves. They're not looking at me, they're looking at my shoes (and quickly away). They're busy staying in touch with consumer culture. What's in and what's out, what's coming and what's gone. Shopping as competition, a sort of a sporting event.

Cities organized on a strip-mall model tend to lack stories which define neighborhoods and homelands. Cures are easy enough to propose. Acting them out is politics.

Governments make decisions that determine what life is like in their city. They don't often provide much in the way of vision. They're usually listening to wheels that squeak loudest—and the howling wheel in Phoenix is profit.

The loudest noises come from developers. Single-class subdivisions and malls—the consumer life ever more commodified—are the tools of their trade. But it does not have to be that way. Citizens can elect people interested in developing and preserving integrated multiclass, multiracial neighborhoods connected by buses and light rail, neighborhoods to which citizens might come to feel a sense of allegiance. It might even happen in an entity so amorphous as Phoenix.

But I should be careful with generalities, the curse of theorizing class. They're always based on unconscious or conscious bias, and partly incorrect.

Millions and millions of people live in greater Phoenix, hundreds of thousands in Tucson and Albuquerque. It's very likely each of those cities has many functional neighborhoods of the kind I'm enthusiastic about. They need to be cherished, not rebuilt.

And, despite what I see as endemic placelessness, Phoenix has striking attractions, like the refrigerated room of kachina dolls at the Heard Museum, four hundred donated by one-time presidential candidate Barry Goldwater. They're arranged in keeping with the order of the Hopi ceremonial calendar, and constitute a wake-up call to those who've never been exposed to the elegance of native imaginative thinking. The Frank Lloyd Wright workshop and home, Taliesin West, was built in the deserts east of Scottsdale, at the end of a long winding two-track road through the cactus, the towers of Phoenix on the horizon. Now it's engulfed by tract houses. I like to imagine Wright out on his patio, making peace with time, the red sun setting over the desert as he aged and watched the canyon wrens.

(Note for readers: To visit anomie in Phoenix a couple of decades ago, read Dennis Johnson's shattering "Angels." A feel for emotional isolations in the Southwest can also be gotten from Leslie Marmon Silko's scattered, fitfully brilliant *Almanac of the Dead: A Novel.* The more surreal qualities of growing up in upscale Tucson are profoundly present in Joy Williams's recent novel *The Quick and the Dead.* And, there are two masterpieces, Silko's *Ceremony* and Cormac McCarthy's *Blood Meridian, Or the Evening Redness in the West.*)

On March 21, 1981, the activist environmental group called Earth First! held its first national gathering at the Glen Canyon Dam. Their gathering was a sort of carnival, and culminated when five of them lugged a massive black bundle out on the dam, and let a tapered, three-hundred-foot streamer of black plastic unfurl down the long concrete face, to create the illusion that the dam was "cracked." That joke established their presence in the national imagination more vividly than any amount of rhetoric.

It was a threat that set off alarms in the Southwest. Crazies were threatening the water supply. It wasn't taken too seriously in New Mexico, where the major population lives near the Rio Grande. But Arizona is mostly an oasis culture. Without water Tucson and Phoenix wither.

Southwestern agriculture involved irrigation before the ancients came to the idea of tillage. Ancient people led water from streams to native plants, which they later harvested. The Papago practiced arroyo mouth irrigation; they led flash floods into catchment basins where cottonwoods, willows, and burro-brushes were planted in rows across a watercourse to slow the current and trap rich silts, and planted quickly germinating tepary beans in tiny irregular fields after a rain, harvesting before the desert soils dried and turned bricklike again. And then, of course, the Hohokam built the first large-scale irrigation project in what's now the United States along the Gila River and the Salt River just south of present-day Phoenix. Their largest canal was eleven miles long, and carried water to irrigate eight thousand acres.

Anglo irrigation began in 1867, with canals along traces of the Hohokam system. After serious feuding over water, the U.S. Reclamation Service was brought in to reorganize and develop the valley. In 1905 they began building a storage dam some sixty miles east of Phoenix. Finished in 1911, Roosevelt Dam was the highest in the world, 280 feet above bedrock, a 10.5-million-dollar project. Some 300,000 acres along the Salt

River were opened to irrigation, and the economy in Phoenix began to cook. By the late 1930s, irrigators were using 95 percent of the waters in the Gila and Salt Rivers and coming up short. And the development of Tucson and Phoenix depended on water. Nobody is interested in a dry oasis. By 1953 Arizona was pumping 4.8 million acre-feet of water from underground, emptying ancient aquifers, a stopgap measure.

So the state went to federal court and came out in 1964 with rights to 2.8 million acre-feet from the Colorado River plus the full flow of its own tributaries. In 1968 the U.S. Congress passed the Colorado River Basin Project Act, which authorized the Central Arizona Project (CAP). Beginning with Parker Dam, on the Colorado, which backed up Lake Havasu, builders tunneled through the Buckskin Mountains so they could dump 1.2 million acre-feet of water into the Granite Reef Aqueduct, which carried it to Orme Dam north of Phoenix, and then south in the Tucson Aqueduct. The total cost for lifting the water some 1,250 feet and carrying it more than 330 miles inland to dampen down the burning valleys around Phoenix and Tucson, was more than three billion dollars. The first water ran through the system in 1985.

Trouble is, water from the canals of the CAP has turned out, because of evaporation, to be saline. And the historically fertile bottomlands in Arizona have already been salinated, the result of salty desert water and inadequate drainage; half have been abandoned. Many farmers want little to do with CAP water. A lot of it goes to recharge aquifers.

Tucson and Phoenix, on the other hand, use enormous expanses of mown grass, lawns and golf courses, faux lakes and giant fountains to draw in tourists and retirees. The crop they raise is development; their economies run on water, which flows toward money. Is it any wonder, then, that the oasis seems increasingly citified?

The grand hotels. Ain't they something? I love the Biltmore, which in so many ways epitomizes Frank Lloyd Wright's idea of an architecture that might help furnish our imaginations with intimations of order. (Wright doesn't get credit for the construction, but it everywhere embodies his vision.) I love parking by the Arizona Canal as the last twilight golfers are putting out. The hotel hovers, telling me that my life can't be insignificant if I get to come here.

Since opening in 1929, not long before the Great Crash, the Biltmore has been a meticulously maintained Southwestern legitimizing dream. We, the story goes, have the Biltmore, and thus we're anybody's equal, in elegance, and in power if you want to think about it so crudely, and in our ability to withstand disappointment. "Bulletproof and invisible," an old tavern haunting friend, long since dead, used to say.

Bruce Berger, in *The Telling Distance: Conversations with the American Desert,* says, "If the forces responsible for the jagged gray ranges around Phoenix had conspired to create, on a dare, some Art Deco cliff dwellings, they might have come up with the Arizona Biltmore.

"The facade, long and recessed, is regularly pocked and shadowed as if colonized by cliff swallows, while the interior seems a flow of elegant, rectilinear caves."

The building does indeed connect to Southwestern land-forms. It sort of epitomized, maybe defined, when it was built, in those days some miles east of Phoenix, Southwestern bajada culture. It's reminiscent of pueblos like Hopi and Taos, which also mirror and reflect.

After locking my automobile, a gesture I find myself enjoying (it identifies me as one of the psychically unwound-able patrons here), and strolling inside as if we sure do belong in this setting, Annick and I claim one of the couches near the piano player, where I love sipping an "up" martini and digging into a crystal bowl of warm Brazil nuts. Later Annick and I wander into shops, where we consider and reject Hermès scarves, and out into the grounds where elaborate and immac-ulate beds of flowers smell in every season of spring.

We covertly study the people who live in the casitas as they come and go and think they're like us, only luckier, and we amble past swimming pools, abandoned for the evening, and smile at the well-to-do children running out of control on the lawns. But we've never gone to Wright's, the signature dining room, for some dish like "Seared Scarlet Snapper served with Piquillo Peppers and Preserved Kumquats." And we've never slept in one of the rooms. We'll eat at the grill, on the patio by the mesquite fire in its big fireplace. Poor us. But we may, one of these times, like a movie star, following in the footsteps of Clark Gable and Lucy Arnaz, rent a casita.

We go the Phoenician, a grandiose marble-floored foolish-ness, for other distractions. I'm a sucker for splendor tempered by heartbreak, stories reeking of contrary ambitions, monied dreamers acting out their aristocratic if semi-nonsensical dreams. Like Gatsby. So, on a terrace, gazing out to the grand and expanding glitter of Phoenix, more martinis, another attempt at timelessness.

Charles Keating, the boy behind the Phoenician, fell from grace in the savings-and-loan fiasco, and so did thousands who trusted him with millions of dollars. Of Keating, in *Blood Orchid: An Unnatural History of America,* Charles Bowden writes, "His brilliance was in his knowing his emptiness, in sensing it and acting on it. He made money meaningless by squandering billions." Hubris, and its rewards or not, as in the *Iliad.* We begin to feel perhaps that we're in a movie.

When I think of consulting a planning expert, trying to figure out which Phoenix fantasies are cooking now, and who's at the stove, who's cooking, I hear that old difficult ghost, Ed Abbey, at my ear, whispering, "Why bother, it'll be bullshit anyhow."

Young coyotes, on a bright morning, ran routes around my new white ball. Sprinklers were sprinkling, the air smelled of fresh cut grass, and there we were, creatures on the fairway, at play. The coyotes ghosted off into a draw where the prickly pear were thick with blossoms the color of tea roses.

Golf runs on simple pleasures. After breathing for a slow moment, I struck one of those occasional shots. It looked to be perfect as it lifted and hung, and fell soundlessly. For a moment it seemed pure, until the air went out of that balloon one more time. My ball was in the back bunker, buried in a coyote track.

EPILOGUE

Mudhead Dreaming

Imagine the problem is that we cannot imagine a future where we possess less but are more.

CHARLES BOWDEN

Blood Orchid: An Unnatural History of America

Gary Paul Nabhan is an arid-lands ethno-botanist and former MacArthur Fellow now located at the University of Northern Arizona in Flagstaff. In *Coming Home to Eat: The Pleasures and Politics of Local Foods,* Nabhan tells us of obesity and adult-onset diabetes among Tohono O'odham and Seri Indians, aberrant blood-sugar and insulin levels as a result of eating fiber-poor junk foods and those provided by the federal-surplus commodities program. The average weight of O'odham men increased from 158 pounds in 1938 to 202 in 1978.

The only widespread control turns out to be a return to traditional native plant foods, which are rich in soluble fiber and fructose, tannins, and other blood sugar-lowering substances. Nabhan quotes a Pima Indian friend, "To be Indian, you gotta eat Indian." The need to rediscover the seeds of lost varieties, and get them back into cultivation and native diets, was formalized in Native Seeds/SEARCH. Nabhan's leadership earned him the MacArthur Fellowship.

Nabhan, I think, is partways an artist at play who enjoys finding foods growing lost under our feet, a joke on our dominant culture's power to control the world. But his essential work is done in concert with others; he continually emphasizes that his work is communal.

Nabhan's worries are interrelated. Obesity and diabetes exist in growing dimensions everywhere. No doubt we should all, not just native peoples, be eating home-grown foods. Yet, as Americans eat more and more processed and prepared foods, conglomerates are buying seed stocks so as to control them worldwide and thus determine what they *can* eat. The world produces huge quantities of unused food and 35,000 people starve to death every day, their deaths often the result of inhumane decisions by "First World" agribusiness.

Priorities, clearly, need some rethinking. But rethinking, if there's any hope for a cutting edge to it, is not likely to come from the World Trade Organization and its bottom-line oriented corporate clients, folks with a serious interest in maintaining the status quo.

On the other hand, thousands and thousands of world citizens, some working alone, others banded together in an almost endless variety of nongovernmental citizens' organizations, are doing what they can to promote justice and preserve ecosystems. Transgressive thinking, as usual, is most likely going on in somebody's kitchen.

In tavern life a ration of chaos is taken to be normal. The world encountered by hunters and gatherers is also understood to be unpredictable. It's accepted that events are governed by the laws of chance. As a consequence their myths tend to be about tricksters and sly transformational creators—coyotes, ravens, or hunchbacked Kokopelli dancing around and playing his flute, stories about the pleasures of surprise, the joke of living successfully.

Settled agricultural people, on the other hand, as in the Southwestern pueblos, see chaos as randomness, confusion, and incoherence that existed at the time of creation. Their primary myths tend to be stories about progressing toward order. They regard unpredictability as an evil to be fought at all costs. Alfonso Ortiz, writing about the village where he grew up, says, "This quest for and tradition of peace has imbued the lives of the San Juan people with a sense of ultimate sanctuary, with a belief that there are places so sacred that one can be safe from harm while there."

But pueblo people also want the rains to fall. And however reluctantly, they are forced to recognize that events outside the pueblo will never be entirely predictable, and that the world inside the pueblo can grow blind-eyed, make mistakes, and need correcting, that some fracturing may occasionally be necessary in order to facilitate reseeing.

Opening doors, undercutting received opinion, letting in air, sticking pins into sacred balloons, irreverence, refusing to go on being somebody else's baby—they're life affirming. The

Hopi and the Zuni and other pueblos know this and include mudhead mockery, tricksters, chaos, in their sacred ceremonies. As did and do the Yaqui in their sacred deer dance.

Thinking accurately, thus surviving, depends on our ability to recognize what's really going on instead of what's supposed to be going on, and on that basis to rethink our most basic relationships—to one another and where we live. Stories and the arts help us see, as Coleridge says, by "disassociating the sensibilities," fracturing the ordinary. Chemicals, alcohol, and other drugs often figure in shamanistic traditions. But as we so sadly know, they can lead to disassociations which are beyond useless into tragically dysfunctional.

What are frolics for? Mikhail Bakhtin, the Russian sociopolitical theorist, says, "Carnival celebrated temporary liberation from the prevailing truth and established order; it marked the suspension of all hierarchical rank, privileges, norms, and prohibitions." Pleasure seeking, the upsetting of apple carts, recognitions and reversals, casting off our official personas (game faces which feel like sanctioned straightjackets) may be related activities.

Carnivals, Bahktin writes, are feasts of "becoming, change and renewal." We break patterns so as to free ourselves, move on. Most of us, when we feel secure, enjoy liberation from the repetitions of established order. We embrace psychic and social change and renewal. During medieval carnivals, Bakhtin writes, "all were considered equal. People were, so to speak, reborn to new, purely human relations."

The arts of carnival can be considered techniques for bloodless uprisings. During a carnival we take off and put on masks, real or metaphoric, trying to sense what it would be like if we were someone else.

Carnivals are political events. Permissiveness is all; we celebrate otherness, and bring down the elegant or mighty through mockery and satire. And what are parties, the good ones, but private carnivals? We go out, we travel, with the deliberate intention of re-seeing, rethinking. Travel can be a fracturing ritual, a version of carnival, the fleshly feast, the party.

Useful stories are reaffirming while simultaneously fracturing. They remind us of who and what we are, an evolving creature who's profoundly dependent on the good will of others. They remind us to stay alert because our relationships, if only to ourselves, must be constantly, all day, every day, reinvented.

Ceremonies can work the same way, as with the Yaqui or in the pueblo villages. So stories, parties, ceremonies laced with humor, parody, humiliations, triumphs, profanations, mudhead clowning, crowning and uncrowning, all helping us to see, and evolve.

As early as the seventh century B.C., clowns wandered the marketplaces of Greece, lampooning soldiers and slaves, senators, and even idiots and gods. Political and social satire evolved into dramatic comedy, an occasionally profound art, as in Aristophanes. The Fool, as jester in medieval courts, said the unsayable, scattered anarchy, allowing nobility and kings to laugh at and see through their otherwise untouchable personas. The Fool is essential in King Lear, and Falstaff is an emblematic figure we recognize in taverns today.

In the early eleventh century, the Roma began leaving their homelands in Tajikistan and northern India, and made their way to Europe around the year 1300, telling fortunes, among other things, with Tarot decks featuring one unnumbered card, that of the Fool. They became known as Gypsies, and were popular entertainers in marketplaces and courts all over Europe. Street comedy in Italy evolved into the commedia dell'arte with its stock figures, the Harlequin in patchwork and Pierrot with the elegant white face. Bawdy songs went with the comic skits. In America commedia became vaudeville, the popular public entertainment of the late nineteenth century, formative in the evolution of early jazz, and at the core of classical film comedies.

The Harlequin and his straight man, white-faced Pierrot, we recognize them in Abbot and Costello, in the Marx Brothers and the Three Stooges, in Lucy and Desi. We see the Fool tripping along innocently in Charlie Chaplin and Jerry Lewis, and thwarting the Trickster in "Krazy Kat," and in "Tom and Jerry" and "Roadrunner" cartoons.

Thinking transgressively is clearly an ancient and ongoing cross-cultural necessity. Fools, tricksters, jugglers, Gypsies, mimes, jugglers, contemporary mudheads and their flute-playing humpbacked predecessors, the Kokopelli, and surreal half-animal figures painted into Mimbres bowls, all of them sacred while at play—their wit fragments the ordinary.

Maybe we could use ironic mouthy mudheads wandering around the halls of the U.S. Congress. Think of the Beatles and Dylan and hard-time rock-and-roll and Thomas Jefferson, who said, "I hold it a little rebellion now and then is a good thing, and as necessary in the political world as storms in the physical."

Seeking homelands, we come and go, always hoping to nest in. We need and yearn to believe. Yet in order to survive we need to be deflated, and driven to continually start over by reexamining what we believe. Humor is a door to insight, and a survival skill. It is said that language was the singular human discovery. But maybe not, maybe it was laughter.

Rethinking is going on all around the world, and preconceptions are changing, rapidly. Sacredness, recently, has actually been a consideration in economic decisions. For example, consider this problem, and this solution, which would never have had a chance without citizen values, and pressure.

The problem: Crop engineers have inserted a hybrid maize with genes from *Bacillus thuringiensis,* a soil microbe toxic to a number of corn pests. But the pollen of what's called Bt corn is toxic to monarch butterfly larvae. And 80 percent of the monarchs which overwinter in the mountains of central Mexico begin life in the Corn Belt.

In Mexico, going to see the monarchs a couple of years ago, Annick and I were on dusty trails at an elevation of over ten thousand feet, alongside fathers carrying their children, pregnant women and grandmothers, old men with crutches, all marching or struggling along to pay homage to the hundreds of millions of clustered butterflies. Alison Hawthorne Deming, who teaches at the University of Arizona, in a book of poems, *The Monarchs,* says,

> *From the village tourists ride*
> *in cattle trucks up to the El Rosario site,*
> *swimming, on warm days, through*

a tide of evanescent fluttering.
If you go there—no gathering jar,
no ether, no pins, no net—spend money wildly,
placing your wealth in the hands
of the ejiditarios, which means
you place it in the wings of the monarchs,
in the family album of earth's history
that their brief lives exalt.

Deming is acknowledging another threat to the monarchs—poverty. Forests where the monarchs overwinter are threatened by logging on the part of local peasants. What to do? What good are our powers if we can't find the wit or will to support those poor people while preserving a species so redolent with life?

The solution: In December 2001, President Vincente Fox announced that a 6.1-million-dollar monarch trust formed by the Mexican government and a group of private foundations will pay locals to stop cutting trees and to reforest. So economic support to the poor and preservation of an environmental treasure. Let's hope the Mexican government sees it through.

About three years back, Gary Nabhan took Annick and me on a trip to the Mexican village of Cucurpe, to visit families he got to know while doing graduate work there in 1976. Nabhan hired a couple of the farmers, and they came to Tucson, to the Arizona-Sonora Desert Museum where he was then director of Science, and put on an exhibition of pit-roasting sword-leafed agave *(Agave lechuguilla)*. But the part of the trip I like to think about involves the mescal, the legendary booze with a worm floating at the bottom, that those farmers sold us in Cucurpe, all that we could legally get over the border. Nabhan was driving, so I got to sipping and drifted into a dream of finding I was at that moment home, coming home and going home.

Vast creosote flatlands, saguaro on bajadas, timbered snow-topped mountains, Navajo hogans among the red-rock mesas, glittering cities, barrios, nuclear workshops, smugglers along the borderlands, unemployed cowhands—where have we been, where is the Southwest going? That will of course depend on the will of citizens there. It's a matter of vision. What do they want, what do they imagine as a future worth working for? Who's doing the inventing, the dreaming up?

People don't want to be called intellectuals, it sounds elitist. But some of them are, for instance Ed Abbey and Bill Eastlake and Doug Peacock and Gary Paul Nabhan. Others I've admired are Leslie Marmon Silko and William deBuys, Sharman Apt Russell and Richard Shelton and Simon Ortiz, Luci Tapahonso and Ron Carlson and Alison Deming, Carla Elling and Alberto Ríos, Keith Wilson and Scott Momaday and Jimmy Santiago Baca and Joy Harjo, Charles Bowden and Fred Turner, Ann Zwinger, Dave Foreman and Barbara Kingsolver. Pray for me, whom have I forgotten? Thousands. May they forgive me. But anyway, that's a list of Southwesterners from my profession who've acted as if they think the well-being of the Southwest is a personal project. Others include pinstripe lawyers and lonesome cowgirls, beatniks and grocery-store clerks who've enriched their homeland by insisting on spreading equality around and taking care of ecologies, human and otherwise. Maybe there's a billionaire. Homelands are mostly made, I think, of reverence and intentions.

Saints and fools have always been out to undercut hierarchies and break open ripe melons for all to enjoy. But as we know, in the long run everybody has to see this deal through for themselves.

William Kittredge has published fiction and essays in such magazines as *The Atlantic Monthly, Harper's, Rolling Stone, Outside, TriQuarterly, North American Review,* and *Iowa Review.* A graduate of the Iowa Writers' Workshop and a professor of creative writing at the University of Montana, Kittredge's works include *Hole in the Sky: A Memoir, Owning It All: Essays,* and the story collections *The Van Gogh Fields and Other Stories* and *We Are Not in This Together.*

This book is set in Garamond 3, designed by
Morris Fuller Benton and Thomas Maitland
Cleland in the 1930s, and Monotype Grotesque,
both released digitally by Adobe.

Printed by R. R. Donnelley and Sons on
Gladfelter 60-pound Thor Offset smooth
white antique paper.

Dust jacket printed by Miken Companies.
Color separation by Quad Graphics.

Three-piece case of Ecological Fiber garnet
side panels with Sierra black book cloth as the
spine fabric. Stamped in Lustrofoil metallic silver.